Battered
Women

OTHER BOOKS OF RELATED INTEREST

Battered Women

Lane Volpe, *Book Editor*

Bruce Glassman, *Vice President*
Bonnie Szumski, *Publisher*
Helen Cothran, *Managing Editor*
Brenda Stalcup, *Series Editor*

Contemporary Issues

Companion

GREENHAVEN
PRESS ®

THOMSON

™

GALE

San Diego • Detroit • New York • San Francisco • Cleveland
New Haven, Conn. • Waterville, Maine • London • Munich

© 2004 by Greenhaven Press. Greenhaven Press is an imprint of The Gale Group, Inc., a division of Thomson Learning, Inc.

Greenhaven® and Thomson Learning™ are trademarks used herein under license.

For more information, contact
Greenhaven Press
27500 Drake Rd.
Farmington Hills, MI 48331-3535
Or you can visit our Internet site at http://www.gale.com

LIBRARY OF CONGRESS CATALOGING-IN-PUBLICATION DATA

Battered women / Lane Volpe, book editor.
  p. cm. — (Contemporary issues companion)
  Includes bibliographical references and index.
  ISBN 0-7377-1617-7 (lib. : alk. paper) — ISBN 0-7377-1618-5 (pbk. : alk. paper)
    1. Wife abuse—United States. 2. Abused women—United States. 3. Abused women—Legal status, laws, etc.—United States. I. Volpe, L. Carl (Lane Carl), 1951– . II. Series.
  HV6626.2.B275 2004
  362.82'92'0973—dc22   2003056877

Printed in the United States of America

CONTENTS

FOREWORD

In the news, on the streets, and in neighborhoods, individuals are confronted with a variety of social problems. Such problems may affect people directly: A young woman may struggle with depression, suspect a friend of having bulimia, or watch a loved one battle cancer. And even the issues that do not directly affect her private life—such as religious cults, domestic violence, or legalized gambling—still impact the larger society in which she lives. Discovering and analyzing the complexities of issues that encompass communal and societal realms as well as the world of personal experience is a valuable educational goal in the modern world.

Effectively addressing social problems requires familiarity with a constantly changing stream of data. Becoming well informed about today's controversies is an intricate process that often involves reading myriad primary and secondary sources, analyzing political debates, weighing various experts' opinions—even listening to first-hand accounts of those directly affected by the issue. For students and general observers, this can be a daunting task because of the sheer volume of information available in books, periodicals, on the evening news, and on the Internet. Researching the consequences of legalized gambling, for example, might entail sifting through congressional testimony on gambling's societal effects, examining private studies on Indian gaming, perusing numerous websites devoted to Internet betting, and reading essays written by lottery winners as well as interviews with recovering compulsive gamblers. Obtaining valuable information can be time-consuming—since it often requires researchers to pore over numerous documents and commentaries before discovering a source relevant to their particular investigation.

Greenhaven's Contemporary Issues Companion series seeks to assist this process of research by providing readers with useful and pertinent information about today's complex issues. Each volume in this anthology series focuses on a topic of current interest, presenting informative and thought-provoking selections written from a wide variety of viewpoints. The readings selected by the editors include such diverse sources as personal accounts and case studies, pertinent factual and statistical articles, and relevant commentaries and overviews. This diversity of sources and views, found in every Contemporary Issues Companion, offers readers a broad perspective in one convenient volume.

In addition, each title in the Contemporary Issues Companion series is designed especially for young adults. The selections included in every volume are chosen for their accessibility and are expertly edited in consideration of both the reading and comprehension levels of the audience. The structure of the anthologies also enhances accessibility. An introductory essay places each issue in context and provides helpful facts such as historical background or current statistics and legislation that pertain to the topic. The chapters that follow organize the material and focus on specific aspects of the book's topic. Every essay is introduced by a brief summary of its main points and biographical information about the author. These summaries aid in comprehension and can also serve to direct readers to material of immediate interest and need. Finally, a comprehensive index allows readers to efficiently scan and locate content.

The Contemporary Issues Companion series is an ideal launching point for research on a particular topic. Each anthology in the series is composed of readings taken from an extensive gamut of resources, including periodicals, newspapers, books, government documents, the publications of private and public organizations, and Internet websites. In these volumes, readers will find factual support suitable for use in reports, debates, speeches, and research papers. The anthologies also facilitate further research, featuring a book and periodical bibliography and a list of organizations to contact for additional information.

A perfect resource for both students and the general reader, Greenhaven's Contemporary Issues Companion series is sure to be a valued source of current, readable information on social problems that interest young adults. It is the editors' hope that readers will find the Contemporary Issues Companion series useful as a starting point to formulate their own opinions about and answers to the complex issues of the present day.

INTRODUCTION

In November 1987, six-year-old Lisa was brutally beaten to death by her adoptive father, Joel Steinberg. At Steinberg's trial, widespread condemnation was directed at Lisa's adoptive mother, Hedda Nussbaum, a battered woman who failed to intervene on Lisa's behalf or summon medical personnel in an attempt to save her daughter's life. Nussbaum quickly became a high-profile, if controversial, symbol of battered women across the nation. While her failure to protect her children created a public outcry, her case did draw public attention to the isolation and torture that accompany the most severe cases of domestic abuse. Such physical and psychological torture, doctors and psychiatrists testified, left Nussbaum mentally and physically crippled, incapable of defending either herself or her children from Steinberg's heinous abuse. This case is characteristic of the tragedy and destruction caused by battering, a crime which directly affects an estimated 6 million women per year and brings devastation to families, communities, and the nation as a whole.

While men can be victims of domestic violence, the overwhelming majority of cases involve abuse of women at the hands of their male partners or spouses. According to statistics from the U.S. Bureau of Justice, approximately one-third of female murder victims are killed by a current or former intimate partner, compared to only 4 percent of male murder victims. Furthermore, while the number of women killed by an intimate partner has been increasing since 1995, the proportion of male victims has been decreasing. Women ages thirty-five to forty-nine are the most likely to be killed by an intimate partner, while women from sixteen to twenty-four are the most vulnerable to nonfatal domestic violence. In recent years, attention has been drawn to lesbian victims of domestic violence, a group of battered women who have been historically overlooked and underserved. Statistics reveal that domestic violence occurs in same-sex relationships at a rate roughly equal to that of domestic violence against heterosexual women. Because battered women from all walks of life are often reluctant to report abuse, these national figures may greatly underestimate the true prevalence of domestic violence. But even based on the conservative figures available, it is clear that domestic violence seriously affects many women throughout the country, no matter their race, ethnicity, socioeconomic status, or sexual orientation.

Donna Shalala, former secretary of the U.S. Department of Health and Human Services, has referred to domestic violence as an "unacknowledged epidemic" in society. Indeed, the collective costs of battering affect each and every member of society, regardless of whether or not they have personally experienced domestic violence. Costs associated with medical care, counseling, emergency housing, and the criminal justice system make domestic violence a very expensive social problem. Domestic violence can also lead to other social problems, such as homelessness. According to Delaware Senator Joseph Biden, at least half of all homeless women and children end up on the streets because they are trying to escape violence in their homes. Additionally, the overall economic effect of domestic violence on society is exacerbated by the indirect costs associated with missed workdays and decreased productivity among battered women in the workforce.

Despite the collective costs of domestic violence, society has long held the belief that violence in the home is a personal matter that should be handled privately by the individuals involved. In the past, law enforcement officers often provided little protection for battered women; instead, they would simply instruct the couple to work out their differences once they both calmed down. It was not until the 1960s that public attitudes toward domestic violence began to change, primarily through the efforts of the feminist movement. Feminists and other social activists pointed out that if a man beat up a stranger in the street, he would go to jail, but if he inflicted the same physical damage to his wife in their home, he rarely would be punished. These activists argued that by not taking domestic violence seriously, the police and the legal system were denying battered women equal protection under the law. As a result, during the latter part of the twentieth century, law enforcement agencies and the legal system started to treat domestic violence much more seriously. For example, many police departments have undertaken special training programs to teach officers effective methods for dealing with abuse cases, and judges increasingly hand down tough sentences to convicted batterers.

Another outcome of the rise in public awareness over the last few decades has been the establishment of numerous social services to assist victims of domestic violence. Battered women's shelters—which provide victims with support, counseling, and a safe place to live—can be found in many communities throughout the nation. Other programs are designed to help battered women in navigating the legal system, obtaining medical care, and reentering the workforce. The most successful interventions, experts maintain, are those that involve the cooperative efforts of diverse social service agencies to address the various needs of battered women. In addition, more agencies now focus not only on the victim but also on the abuser, offering batterer intervention programs to help men change their behavior. Finally, many programs stress the importance of educating children and teenagers about the realities of domestic violence in hopes that fewer boys will grow up to become batterers and fewer girls to become victims.

Perhaps the most comprehensive and significant remedy to the problem of domestic violence has been the passage of the federal Violence Against Women Act (VAWA) of 1994, followed by a second version of the act (VAWA II) signed into law in 2000. According to Lenore Walker, a psychologist and national expert on battered women, the VAWA declares "violence against women to be a civil rights violation—in other words, a violation of every woman's right to be protected under the United States constitution." By making violence against women a civil rights complaint, the VAWA enables battered women to file for damages against their abusers in federal court without adhering to the usual time limits. The act also grants federal funds to local and state police departments for better training in the protection of victims of domestic violence, with receipt of the funding contingent on a strict adherence to a policy of prosecuting batterers. Because many of the original act's provisions were set to expire in October 2000, VAWA II was created, reauthorizing a number of the grant programs begun under the first VAWA. In addition, the second act provides funds to programs that address intimate partner violence on college campuses, offer civil and legal services to victims, and improve access to services for battered immigrant women.

Through the passage of the two Violence Against Women Acts, Congress clearly signaled that domestic violence is a serious crime, one that deserves a place on the national policy agenda because it affects society as a whole. In the words of New York Senator Hillary Rodham Clinton, "If women are free from violence, their families will flourish. . . . And when families flourish, communities and nations will flourish." *Battered Women: Contemporary Issues Companion* examines current efforts to achieve this goal. The authors provide a comprehensive overview of the problem, discuss the effectiveness of various legal and social remedies, and present the personal stories of individuals whose lives have been touched by domestic violence.

CHAPTER 1

VIOLENCE AGAINST WOMEN: AN OVERVIEW

Contemporary Issues
Companion

THE NATURE OF DOMESTIC VIOLENCE

L. Elisabeth Beattie and Mary Angela Shaughnessy

L. Elisabeth Beattie is a writer-in-residence and associate professor of English at Midway College in Midway, Kentucky. Mary Angela Shaughnessy, a Sister of Charity of Nazareth, is the university legal counsel and head of the doctoral program in educational leadership at Spalding University in Louisville, Kentucky. In the following selection from their book *Sisters in Pain: Battered Women Fight Back*, Beattie and Shaughnessy provide an overview of the nature of domestic violence. The authors discuss the prevalence of abuse, describe risk factors associated with battering, and examine societal attitudes that promote violence against women. Society must overcome stereotypes of battered women as passive and weak, argue Beattie and Shaughnessy, in order to understand the true nature of domestic violence and to address the actual needs of battered women.

Pick up almost any newspaper or magazine, flip through radio news reports or television feature specials, and sooner or later you'll encounter the facts. One in four women in the United States is raped during her lifetime, and only one rape in eleven is reported. In 1997, according to the U.S. Bureau of Justice Statistics, 4.5 million violent acts against women occurred, and 95 percent of the perpetrators were men. The U.S. Justice Department's most recent statistics suggest that 30 percent of the 1,414 women murdered in 1992 were killed by their husbands, ex-husbands, or boyfriends. Annually, spouses and significant others commit 13,000 acts of violence against women in U.S. workplaces, a figure that translates into five billion dollars each year in medical expenses, catapulting domestic violence into the number-one cause for women seeking treatment in hospital emergency rooms.

And just what is domestic violence? Various individuals, institutions, and organizations articulate different definitions, but suffice it to say that the first widespread definitions of spousal abuse offered in the United States in the 1970s focused on physical violence and its increased frequency. Twenty years later, the National Coalition against Domestic Violence cited domestic violence as *"a pattern of behavior* with the effect of establishing power and control over another person through fear and intimidation. Battering happens when batterers believe they are entitled to control their partners, when violence is permissible, when violence will produce the desired effect or prevent a worse one, and when the benefits outweigh the consequences."

But no matter its specific manifestations, a significant fact publicized by the National Coalition against Domestic Violence is that "more than 50 percent of all women will experience some form of violence from their spouses during marriage. More than one-third [approximately 18 million women] are battered repeatedly every year."

Domestic Violence in Historical Perspective

Yet it's important to note that abuse of women, although epidemic, isn't new. Western civilization documents the medieval comments of Geoffrey de la Tour de Landry concerning how to punish the "wickedness of a nagging wife." In 1371 he wrote, "Here is an example to every good woman that she suffer and endure patiently, nor strive with her husband nor answer him before strangers, as did once a woman who did answer her husband before strangers with short words: and he smote her with his fist down to earth; and then with his foot he struck her in her visage and broke her nose, and all her life after she had her nose crooked, which so shent [spoiled] and disfigured her visage after, that she might not for shame show her face, it was so foul blemished. And this she had for her language that she was wont to say to her husband, and therefore the wife ought to suffer, and let the husband have the words, and to be master for that is her duty."

Less than fifty years later, Bernard of Sienna, Italy, suggested that men treat their spouses with the same affection that they show their livestock, a suggestion still regarded, statistics would suggest, as novel by contemporary U.S. culture, which provides three times as many shelters for animals as for abused women. In colonial America, a more compassionate culture applied what was later called the "rule of thumb" to situations necessitating the chastisement of wayward wives. Lawmakers still condoned husbands beating their spouses but determined they should do so only with sticks the width of their thumbs.

Cross-Cultural Perspectives

Historically, Eastern and African cultures have also abused women. Even today, as has been the case for centuries, grooms burn to death brides who are unable to deliver the dowries that their grooms demand. Recent estimates reveal that in India one such woman is killed every twelve hours. Official police records attribute 4,835 females' deaths in 1990 to murder by their disgruntled fiancés, a number that doesn't come close to capturing the thousands of Indian women who succumb annually to "accidental burns."

Iraqi men often kill female relatives who they even suspect of adultery; Mali and Sudanese men practice female circumcision, an opera-tion performed without anesthesia that results in severe pain, persis-tent infections, and, frequently, death; and the ancient Chinese proverb, "A wife married is like a pony bought; I'll ride her and whip her as I like," was echoed halfway around the world as recently as 1987 by the comment in a Papua, New Guinea, parliamentary debate that "wife beating is an accepted custom; we are wasting our time debating the issue."

Patriarchal societies, cultures controlled by men, have traditionally evoked religious doctrine, from translations of the Bible to the teach-ings of the Koran, to justify battering women. But in the past twenty years, the first social-scientific studies of domestic violence have also identified poverty, marital age (that is, men who marry younger), gen-der roles, excessive alcohol consumption, stress, having been abused one's self, and having been raised in or currently residing in a subcul-ture of violence as contributors to, if not causes of, the behavior of numerous batterers. And although it is true that women, as well as men, abuse their partners, a 1992 report to the U.S. Senate Judiciary Committee estimated that of the 1.37 million domestic violence offenses recorded in 1991, 83 percent of the victims were women. The Bureau of Justice Statistics (BJS) stated in its 1995 publication *Violence Against Women: Estimates from the Redesigned Survey* that women expe-rience an average of 1 million more violent victimizations annually than do men. And, as reprehensible as is any form of abuse perpetu-ated by members of either sex against members of their own or of the opposite sex, the overwhelming prevalence of battering of women by men suggests a focus for comprehending and for attempting to allevi-ate dysfunctional relationships based on emotional, physical, and sex-ual control. . . .

In his 1997 book, *Rural Woman Battering and the Justice System: An Ethnography*, British sociologist Neil Websdale, who studied domestic violence in rural Kentucky, wrote that "[early] research shows that woman battering is as likely to occur in urban as it is in rural areas. . . . Survey research in Kentucky also demonstrates that there are few differences between urban and rural rates of woman battering, except that rural battered women report a statistically greater likelihood of being 'shot at,' 'tortured,' and having their 'hair pulled.'" Additional data, including research by Murray Straus, director of the Family Research Laboratory at the University of New Hampshire, and the Sec-ond National Family Violence Survey (1992), reveal spousal abuse to be practiced more in poorer than in wealthier (be they rural or urban) households. The latter study revealed that families with incomes at or below the poverty level experience a 500 percent greater rate of domestic violence than do their wealthier counterparts. The difficulty of verifying such statistics centers on the fact that abuse victims—ashamed of experiences, injuries, and relationships for which their batterers have convinced them they are responsible and afraid of repercussions from their batterers—often underreport and deny their problems. Wealthier victims, who are also often more educated, generally possess greater and easier access to private physicians, to alternative living arrangements, to information concerning social service and legal aid, and, of course, to money, all of which allow them more opportunity to conceal or escape their abuse. These findings, however, do not and should not suggest that educational and financial advantages generally available to a group are physically or psychically in reach of all of its members. While the numbers of poor women who experience abuse appear to exceed the numbers of economically advantaged women who are abused, battering can affect all women, regardless of their economic status, age, race, geographical location, religion, or level of education, just as domestic violence shatters each of its victims by stripping her of any role or status until little of her self remains.

Subcultures of Violence

It stands to reason, and most researchers agree, that a person's need to dominate intimates with threats and violence tends to decrease in proportion to that person's increased income, education, and interpersonal skills. Men raised in environments to which sociologists refer as subcultures of violence, families and communities that approve physical force as a means of coercion, are more likely to batter than are men taught alternative values. In her *Washington Post* article, "Poor Women Experience High Level of Abuse," journalist Sandra G. Boodman also emphasized the striking connection between poverty and violence. She cited findings reported in the April 1998 issue of *Orthopsychiatry* that revealed that poor women especially "experience extraordinarily high levels of severe physical and sexual abuse." She wrote that 83 percent of the 436 women with below-poverty-level incomes who were surveyed in this six-year federally funded study, which she deemed "the most extensive investigation into the physical and emotional health" of such women to date, had survived physical or sexual abuse.

Significant, too, is the fact that even though research has linked binge drinking of alcohol, as well as amphetamine use, to violent behavior, cross-cultural studies of the relationship between drinking and violence indicate that social expectations, more than such substances themselves, determine their users' actions. . . .

The Pervasiveness of Domestic Violence

Certainly, domestic violence surrounds us. And, ironically, physical and sexual (in combination with psychological) crimes against women are—even if the economically disadvantaged among us remain at greater risk—equal-opportunity acts. Regardless of their geographical location, race, age, or economic status, each year, at the rate of one woman every nine seconds, women are attacked by their partners, causing "battering by an intimate partner to be the single most frequent cause of injury to women in the United States," [as reported in *I Am Not Your Victim: Anatomy of Domestic Violence*, edited by Beth Sipe and Evelyn J. Hall]. As contemporary society achieves increasing levels of technological sophistication, our information overload includes overwhelming evidence of the pervasiveness of this barbarism that we still struggle harder to ignore than to banish.

Survivors of such violence tend to keep silent. Abusers assure their victims that the violence that they experience is their—the victims'—fault. Eventually, abuse survivors are so beaten emotionally as well as physically that they believe their batterers' excuses. And, when women are abused, people who know them often ignore them. Too terrified to risk involvement, family and friends turn away. Also, ironically, when women are battered, it is the people who don't know them who condemn them the most. An ignorant public perceives battered women to be weak because they "permit" themselves to be tortured. Such pundits call battered women passive and pathetic if they cannot escape their abusers. Battered women could, strangers say, leave, if only they had backbones, if only they would assume responsibility for their fates.

Do battered women frighten us? Certainly, they can anger us. And, apparently, it is easier to pass judgment on abuse survivors than it is to censure abusers, just as it is simpler to turn away from than to confront the complicated faces of abuse. After all, individual cases of battering, if uncovered and contemplated, could mirror other, more familiar conflicts, conflicts closer to home.

It is interesting to note that the predictors of batterers' behavior do not appear to exist for the women whom they abuse. Researchers Gerald Hotaling and David Sugarman, who analyzed four hundred cases of domestic violence, report in their *Journal of Family Violence* article, "A Risk Marker Analysis of Assaulted Wives" (1990), that before their abuse, women cannot be distinguished from their nonabused counterparts. Neither personality traits, age, race, educational level, occupation, number of years in a relationship, nor number of children serve as signals to target women most likely to be abused. And, Hotaling and Sugarman discovered that, unlike men who become batterers, even women who witnessed abuse of one parent by another or who were themselves abused as children do not necessarily gravitate, as adults, to abusive relationships. Not all researchers agree with these authors' findings that a woman's prior victimization retains little or no correlation to any subsequent abusive relationships that she may experience. But a significant aspect of Hotaling and Sugarman's research remains their emphasis that a woman's low or lack of self-esteem may be a consequence, rather than a cause, of her battering.

Battered Women Who Kill Their Abusers

An increasing phenomenon related to abuse that is not so much recent as recently publicized is that of female survivors of abuse striking back by assaulting or killing their abusers. But as Evelyn J. Hall, a licensed marriage and family therapist who also serves as clinical supervisor of the Counseling Office for Temporary Assistance for Domestic Crisis (TADC) in Las Vegas, Nevada, wrote in her essay, "The Counselor's Perspective," in *I Am Not Your Victim: Anatomy of Domestic Violence*, edited by Beth Sipe and Evelyn J. Hall, "A battered woman usually kills only in self-defense after prolonged severe abuse; she usually has no intent to kill." In the same essay, Hall added, "Typically, a battered woman who remains in a violent relationship for a long period of time is viewed as weak-willed, masochistic, lacking intelligence, or all three. In fact, the opposite is true. She could not survive the years of abuse if she did not have great strength and resourcefulness."

Hall noted that abused women who kill their batterers tend to have "made frequent calls to police agencies for help," but she added that "[trust] in social service providers, healthcare (both physical and mental) professionals, and judicial system representatives is difficult for a woman who has turned to such agents—often repeatedly—to little or no avail." And even though an estimated "22% to 35% of women seen in emergency rooms annually have been injured by battery," Hall wrote that "the medical community has frequently failed to notice, comment on, or intervene in obvious cases of domestic violence."

From a therapist's viewpoint, Hall said that counseling an abused woman who has killed her batterer "often [focuses] on . . . her legal defense. In most cases," Hall wrote, "the woman is charged with first-degree murder, even though she has no past criminal record." Pointing out the emotional complications of such a client's arrest and of the legal proceedings surrounding her case, Hall wrote, "One issue is how police have treated her. . . . This treatment by the justice system when a woman acts in self-defense extends the wound created by the abuse." She also commented, "The counselor is likely to observe the most severe symptoms of PTSD [post-traumatic stress disorder] as the woman struggles to deal with her shame, degradation, terror, remorse, and anguish about all that has transpired."

Post-traumatic stress disorder, of which battered woman syndrome (BWS) is a part, is a psychological condition that prohibits people who have experienced extreme fear from distinguishing whether or not a threat remains present. Such individuals, who may otherwise maintain normal psychological profiles, suffer flashbacks of the violence they survived, memories that, because they grow more vivid and painful each time they're revisited, are eventually revised or erased by a form of subconscious, self-protective amnesia. But the "forgetting" that reduces a victim's stress, thereby allowing her to cope, also tends to limit her ability to envision alternatives or to always make what people unable to comprehend her position might deem wise choices. Long-term decision making, stressed Lenore Walker, author of *Terrifying Love: Why Battered Women Kill and How Society Responds*, among other landmark works on the topic, becomes almost impossible for women who, to survive, have been forced to shift their focus from planning their futures to surviving the moment. Walker pointed out that the learned helplessness manifested by most survivors of abuse is the aspect of PTSD that distinguishes sufferers of battered woman syndrome. Because such women suffer abuse no matter what their actual behavior, they learn to regard the outcomes of their own actions, rather than their batterers' behavior, as unreliable. Over time, the increasingly distorted perceptions that permit battered women to develop acute short-term survival skills also cause their perspectives to narrow.

Domestic Violence Reflects Societal Problems

Some scholars, such as Lee Bowker in his article "A Battered Woman's Problems are Social, Not Psychological" in *Current Controversies*, object to the theory that abused women suffer learned helplessness on the ground that domestic violence results from systemic societal, as opposed to individual psychological, dysfunction. Labeling abused women as helpless, argued Bowker and others, serves only to revictimize individuals who, in reality, demonstrate sophisticated survival skills.

But as domestic violence scholars Evan Stark and Anne Flitcraft suggest in their book, *Women at Risk*, battered women's behavior, like the behavior of their batterers, is probably best and most accurately understood as a phenomenon at once social and psychological created together by the partners in abusive relationships and their social networks. To admit that abuse cripples its victims psychologically and physically in covert as well as in overt ways, often for a lifetime, does not and should not negate abuse survivors' awesome emotional and spiritual strength. Because survival, by definition, depends on transcending trauma, eliminating the concept and the terms *victim* and *victimization* from discussion of abuse trivializes, instead of substantiates, battered women and their experiences. . . .

As to why so many battered women do not or, ultimately, cannot leave their abusers, [Northern Illinois University associate professor of sociology Susan L.] Miller said, "The time immediately following the violence is often the hardest . . . for a battered woman to leave, because although [her] bruises may still be fresh, [her abuser's] promises sound even more sweet. It is also the most dangerous time for her to leave. . . . Over 50% of women who leave violent relationships are followed, harassed, or further attacked by their estranged partners. . . . Another study indicates that more than half of the men who killed their wives did so following a separation."

Miller noted that battered women, whose self-esteem has almost always been warped, if not wiped out, by their batterers, retain the desperate need to believe their abusers' promises not to wound them again, even as they attempt to act more in accordance with their batterers' wishes. For abuse victims believe what their batterers preach: that any assaults they experience result from their own imperfect behavior, a viewpoint reinforced by "[police], prosecutors, and judges [who] have routinely trivialized battering of women by men, thus reinforcing the social message that this violent behavior is acceptable, that somehow the woman 'deserved' it, that she provoked his anger, that she could do something if she really wanted to stop it, or that she was trying to garner some attention for herself." She wrote, too, that "[economic] dependency on the abuser is real. Battered women and their children, once they leave the abuser, often face poverty, short-term shelter stays, inadequate long-term housing options for low-income women, and generally inferior housing and marginal financial help . . ., all of which is exacerbated if the woman has minimal job skills and/or dependent children."

Battered Women as Survivors

Most important is Miller's conclusion that the "image of the helpless passive victim, who 'chooses' to remain in an abusive relationship, contributes to stereotypes that belie another truth, namely, that remaining in an abusive relationship can also be viewed as a survival struggle in which a woman is desperately trying to shield her children from harm, maintain daily tasks, and figure out how and when to safely make the break." Miller asked, "What do the acts of resiliency and resistance mean?" And she responded that when society learns to regard women who have been abused as "long-term survivors and crisis-managers" rather than "as passive victims in an unequal power struggle," people will begin to understand battered women's motives and their actual, as opposed to their imagined, choices.

Other issues, such as educating health care professionals to recognize abuse and to provide battered women with service information, such as understanding the effects on children of witnessing battering, such as differentiating between a woman's need to remain with her batterer as her perceived way of protecting her children, and such as the judicial system's determination of her competency regarding custody, are not only significant but also vital. So, too, are such issues regarding battered women's shelters as their adequacy in terms of their availability and in terms of their ability to house not only women but also women with male, as well as female, children.

National Efforts to Help Victims

Across the nation, . . . programs to aid survivors of domestic violence abound. Plastic surgeons have created Face to Face: Domestic Violence Project, a national program that offers free reconstructive surgery to survivors of domestic abuse whose features have been altered by violence. A new federal law prevents domestic violence offenders from owning firearms. In New York City, special courts have been formed to handle domestic violence cases exclusively, and in Washington, D.C., teams of judges, instead of individual judges for each issue involved, now hear domestic violence cases. Philip Morris Companies, Inc., in conjunction with the National Network to End Domestic Violence Fund, have formed a statewide network, Doors of Hope, to provide for battered women's immediate food, clothing, shelter, and counseling needs, as well as to provide employment training. And since 1992 Kentucky's domestic violence laws have been among the nation's most progressive; these laws will realize their integrity when they are recognized and enforced by all of the commonwealth's law enforcers and judges. Public awareness, led by such unprecedented public and private sector alliances as Louisville's Take Back the Night, multiply each year. But until we each understand that domestic violence is not only, *a* problem but *our* problem, our mothers, daughters, sisters, and friends will be assaulted. And, one by one they may, in turn, be forced to fight back.

Changes in Society's Attitude Toward Battered Women

Dawn Bradley Berry

As society becomes increasingly aware of the serious nature of domestic violence, public attitudes about battered women are changing for the better, maintains Dawn Bradley Berry in the following excerpt from *The Domestic Violence Sourcebook*. According to Berry, the highly publicized 1995 criminal trial of O.J. Simpson—which revealed that he had physically abused his former wife, Nicole Brown Simpson—drew the nation's attention to domestic violence as a social epidemic that must not be taken lightly. The most important change, Berry contends, is that society no longer views domestic violence as a private matter between two individuals but as a larger problem that has significant ramifications for the entire community. As a result, she writes, federal, state, and local laws have been changed to strengthen punishments for batterers and to provide law enforcement agencies with better training in dealing with domestic violence. Berry is a writer and lawyer in Los Angeles, California.

Abuse knows no boundaries: racial, ethnic, religious, or socioeconomic. It occurs among the very rich and the very poor, the highly educated and the illiterate, in all parts of the world. As stated in a 1994 *Newsweek* article, the phenomenon is as complicated as it is common.

The Battered/Formerly Battered Women's Task Force of the National Coalition Against Domestic Violence (NCADV) says, "Battering is an issue of crime, health, safety, ethics, politics, systems, choices, economics, and socialization. It is an issue of individual, institutional, and cultural significance." As the task force points out, not only must individual thinking and behavior change if battering is to be stopped, but social and cultural values that allow battering and perpetuate it must change as well.

Ingrained social stereotypes support tolerance of abuse in families. Many people still think most instances of battering are "rare" or

Dawn Bradley Berry, *The Domestic Violence Sourcebook*. Los Angeles: Lowell House, 2000. Copyright © 1995 by NTC/Contemporary Publishing Group. All rights reserved. Reproduced by permission.

"minor" and don't warrant outside "interference." Others feel men are inherently aggressive, and women naturally passive, so abuse is inevitable due to "human nature." Some believe that women who nag, get angry, or speak their own minds "provoke" violence and deserve to be beaten. Battering is viewed as a problem caused by stress or poverty, or limited to the "lower classes."

Throughout history, two persistent assumptions have contributed to society's turning away from domestic violence: first, that it was a minor, private, and/or family matter and, second, that others were helpless to do anything about it. Only recently has society begun to face the unspeakable horror of domestic violence, as images such as photographer Donna Ferrato's portraits of the human beings behind the headlines fill books, magazines, and newspapers with their powerful reminder that these are not statistics—these are people. Yet still we turn away.

In the words of Senator Joseph Biden, "If the leading newspapers were to announce tomorrow a new disease that, over the past year, had afflicted from three to four million citizens, few would fail to appreciate the seriousness of the illness. Yet, when it comes to the three to four million women who are victimized by violence each year, the alarms ring softly."

Is there any good news? Definitely. One thing is certain: As the shocking numbers and stories are made public knowledge, attitudes are changing. People are becoming aware of the widespread nature of domestic violence, its devastating effect on women, men, children, and families, and the tragic consequences of turning away. Unfortunately, it has taken events like the killing of Nicole Brown Simpson and her history of abuse to jar the public's awareness that domestic violence is a serious crime and that the consequences are tragic.

The Legacy of the Simpson Case

When O.J. Simpson was acquitted for the 1994 murder of his ex-wife and her friend in his criminal trial, many feared that the verdict would send a message to abusers that they can get away with murder. Another chilling lesson of the Simpson case is that even when women do everything right, everything society tells them to, they can end up murdered—unless outside intervention by law enforcement, criminal justice, and other community sources takes swift and firm action to stop the batterer. Nicole Brown Simpson wisely kept Polaroids of her battered face and a letter O.J. had written apologizing for (and thereby acknowledging) beating her in a safe deposit box. She told friends and family members what was happening, and gained their support. She divorced Simpson, and called the police when he came to her home and attacked her.

"You never do anything. You always come here and you never arrest him." These words, spoken by Nicole Brown Simpson to police who found her, covered in blood and bruises, crouched behind the hedges on her own property after her ex-husband broke into her home, beat and terrorized her, and threatened to kill her, sum up the failure of the system. Is there any other crime for which we place the responsibility for prevention upon the victim rather than upon the perpetrator? At the time Nicole made this statement, California had a mandatory must-arrest policy for domestic violence cases—but it was ignored. When this fact came to light, many people were outraged. Many feel that if Simpson had been treated as a criminal when Nicole first called the police in 1989—with a harsh fine, mandatory counseling in a long-term batterer's program, and strong condemnation of his behavior by his employers and colleagues—Nicole Brown Simpson and Ron Goldman might still be alive.

And this is the positive lesson that has risen out of this tragedy. Although media coverage of the case was, at times, lurid and overblown, it drew the nation's attention to the fact that domestic violence is a life-threatening crime that must not be taken lightly. Calls to shelters and hotlines have steadily increased as abused women realized that they, too, could be in mortal danger. Dozens, possibly hundreds of new organizations, shelters, and hotlines have sprung up as the magnitude of domestic violence has come to light. October has been declared Domestic Violence Awareness Month. The law, at the federal, state, and local levels, has changed to strengthen penalties against abusers and close loopholes. Police departments have begun taking abuse cases more seriously, implementing new protocols, improved officer training, and tougher sanctions against batterers. Even entities not generally affiliated with the organized efforts against domestic violence have become involved. For example, in 1997, the Seattle Public Housing Authority established a training program to educate its personnel, police officers, and others who work with domestic violence victims. In 1995, Illinois State University added a domestic violence unit to its residential assistant training program. State Farm Insurance, once harshly criticized for denying a woman insurance because she was a victim of family violence, has launched a family abuse prevention campaign.

Also, it is important to remember that while one jury acquitted Simpson of murder, another held him accountable in a civil action for the wrongful deaths of his former wife and her friend. Moreover, discussion of the case has made clear that the Simpson case cannot be considered a "normal" case, indicating what would happen under the same circumstances with a noncelebrity defendant. As prosecutor Marcia Clark has emphasized, the Simpson case was an anomaly. The defendant, unlike most, was virtually unconvictable. As Clark commented in her book, "O.J. Simpson slaughtered two innocent people and he walked free—right past the most massive and compelling body of evidence ever assembled against a criminal defendant." The odds of such an outcome in a case not involving a celebrity and sports hero—especially since the outrage, legal evolution, and change in public attitude—are almost nil.

Domestic Violence Can Affect Anyone

We now know that it is not only the poor, the uneducated, or the underprivileged that suffer the pain of domestic violence. We know that batterers can be successful, handsome, gifted men—even our heroes. We know that wife beating is often treated far too casually by the police. We know that domestic violence is often brushed aside as "a family matter" or "no big deal" by the men who batter, by the criminal justice system, and by the public. We know that women who appear to have ample means of escape through money, intelligence, family, and friends remain trapped in violent relationships. We know that even when they do try to get free and end the relationship, the batterer often won't let go.

Perhaps, most of all, the tragedy of the Simpson family has turned the public eye toward the crisis of domestic violence that has become an epidemic in our nation. America can no longer ignore the fact that domestic violence is extremely common, extremely serious, and potentially deadly. The media have begun to take a broad look at what is going on around the country—both the problem and the solutions. In the first few weeks after murder charges were filed against O.J. Simpson and his prior abuse of his wife made national headlines, hotlines, shelters, and coalitions reported a tidal wave of calls—from victims who want help and from men who want to stop battering.

And this is the good news. People have been touched by the horror of domestic violence, both directly and indirectly. The problem continues, but people are trying—both in their own lives, to escape or repair relationships torn by violence, and in the community, to find out what works, how to use it, and how to make services available to all who need them.

Finding Solutions

So what can be done about a problem that is so complex, so pervasive? Certainly, understanding what causes domestic violence and which families are most at risk helps. Despite the grim statistics, there is plenty of evidence that progress is being made by those working to "wage peace" on the home front. Two respected national studies showed a slight decrease in domestic violence between 1975 and 1985. There is less of a stigma attached to those who admit problems in the family and seek outside help, so violence that was previously hidden is being reported more often.

Perhaps the most important change that has taken place toward stopping domestic violence is the way society views the problem.

Throughout most of America's history, the old adage "A man's home is his castle" reflected the attitude that the home was sacrosanct, not to be invaded or disturbed. Women were expected to solve the problem themselves or simply keep it behind closed doors.

Vestiges of the notion that the home is surrounded by a "zone of privacy" that shields it from the scrutiny of the outside world remain, but public sentiment is gradually changing as people are made aware of how severe and how common violence in the home has become. Finally, domestic violence is being seen more clearly as a serious social problem. Psychologists, social workers, and law enforcement officials are beginning to view family violence as something that can be treated and explained, but never tolerated. And the prevailing sense among professionals and the general public alike is that domestic violence is *everybody's* problem.

A Dual Response to Abuse

What *does* work? A wide variety of sources from various fields—psychologists, judges, law enforcement, sociologists, activists, social workers, and the abuse survivors themselves—almost universally agree on two points. First, domestic violence must be treated as a crime. The abuser should be arrested and removed from the home immediately, and spend at least one night in jail. For many, therapy of some kind often helps, but most counselors agree that abusive men must first experience some real consequences if treatment is to be effective. They need a powerful, immediate demonstration by law enforcement that their behavior is criminal, unacceptable, and intolerable.

Second, all of the community institutions addressing domestic violence and helping the victims in various ways must join in a mutual effort to communicate, cooperate, and work together to prevent and stop violence in families. This includes both those organizations immediately associated with helping victims, such as the police, hospitals, and shelters, as well as those that become involved earlier, later, or on a more peripheral basis, such as the courts, probation/parole officers, schools, churches, mental health providers, child protective agencies, welfare and public housing services, politicians, private organizations, social workers, and physicians. Victims must receive immediate support and information, as well as continuing service, no matter where they turn first for help.

There are two different schools of thought within the domestic violence community as to which of these two vital responses should get priority. Should the first order of business be to punish and restrain the abuser, or to help the victim? Everyone seems to agree that both of these matters must be addressed in any successful program. Those that work the best seem to give nearly equal attention to both concerns, often through coordinated systems that use the same facilities to accomplish both goals. For instance, an offender may spend a night in jail, then come before the judge to be charged with his crime *and* told of the treatment options available. Meanwhile, the arresting officer takes the victim to a hospital. The officer or hospital staff makes sure the woman receives information on shelters and other services available for her in the community. She is put in touch with people who can help her find support groups, social services, and assistance with the court processes she will face.

Coordinating Efforts to Help Victims

When an integrated, ongoing effort is made by a coalition of people and groups to coordinate their efforts and skills, both the system as a whole and each component functions more efficiently. The Miami community has made impressive strides toward curtailing the incidence of domestic violence with model shelter programs and a strong partnership between the police and health care communities and other community organizations. Perhaps because the services that are available grew out of grassroots efforts by women with a great deal of gumption but little money, many communities have found that such an integrated program can be established and run for a surprisingly small amount of funding. This type of system also allows for tremendous flexibility according to the particular needs and structure of each geographic area.

Private individuals and businesses are also getting involved. *Ms.* has pledged to keep the issue of domestic violence in the forefront, with its September/October 1994 issue enclosed in a black cover, listing the names of some of the thousands of women killed by their husbands or male partners since 1990. The magazine also announced its pledge to donate five dollars from each subscription to the Family Violence Prevention Fund. Other private businesses have begun to realize their potential to help stop domestic violence, which also promotes positive public relations. For example, the Marshall's chain of discount stores recently donated a percentage of all sales in its 459 stores on a particular date to the Family Violence Prevention Fund and gave all proceeds from a specially designed holiday pin to the fund as well. In 1994, the U.S. Postal Service announced limited public access to change-of-address information filed by individuals and families. . . .

Various communities have [implemented programs to] attack domestic violence. Many have seen astounding results. Most of the techniques that have proven effective can be emulated by others. Several, led by the Duluth, Minnesota Project, have expanded to provide training seminars, curriculums, videos, books, and various other materials to communities throughout the country wishing to establish or improve programs of their own. Things are changing, but it took us a long time to get here, and there is every sign that our work is just beginning.

Domestic Violence and the Military

Catherine Lutz and Jon Elliston

A professor of anthropology at the University of North Carolina at Chapel Hill, Catherine Lutz studies the way the military affects different aspects of U.S. society, especially race and gender relations. Jon Elliston is a journalist with the *Independent Weekly* in Durham, North Carolina, who writes extensively on issues involving politics and the military. In the following article, the authors describe a series of murders that took place at Fort Bragg, North Carolina, during June and July 2002. In the authors' view, the tragic events at Fort Bragg highlight the extreme prevalence of domestic violence in the military as a whole. Compared to civilians, the wives and girlfriends of soldiers are more likely to be abused and experience more severe forms of violence, they contend. Lutz and Elliston examine how the military institutional values that promote violent behavior and the soldiers' inability to cope with the stresses of war contribute to this increased incidence of domestic violence among military families.

The crusty critic Paul Fussell observed that war is always ironic, because things always end up so far from the glory-trailing myths that help start them. Irony, though, pales beside the fear and anger that now swirl around Fort Bragg, North Carolina, the source of many of the troops sent to Afghanistan. It was there that four soldiers recently confused their wives for the enemy and killed them. Marilyn Griffin was stabbed seventy times and her trailer set on fire, Teresa Nieves and Andrea Floyd were shot in the head, and Jennifer Wright was strangled. All four couples had children, several now orphaned because two of the men shot themselves after killing their wives.

The murders garnered wide attention because three of the soldiers served in Special Operations units that have fought in Afghanistan, and because they clustered over a five-week period in June and July [2002]. The killings have raised a host of questions—about the effect of war on the people who wage it, the spillover on civilians from

Catherine Lutz and Jon Elliston, "Domestic Terror," *Nation*, vol. 275, October 14, 2002, p. 18.

training military personnel to kill, the role of military institutional values and even the possible psychiatric side-effects of an antimalarial drug the Army gives its soldiers. On the epidemic of violence against women throughout the United States and on the role of masculinity and misogyny in both military and civilian domestic violence, however, there has been a deafening silence.

Military officials have focused on marital problems and family stress, and have fiercely contested the notion that domestic violence is a more severe problem in the military than in civilian populations, although the Pentagon has not invested much in finding out what the comparison would look like. One Army-funded study that was done, however, found that reports of "severe aggression" against spouses ran more than three times higher among Army families than among civilian ones in 1998.

Underestimating Domestic Violence in the Military

The military nonetheless maintains that violence against spouses is no more prevalent in the armed forces, arguing that it uses different criteria than civilian authorities for identifying domestic violence, including severe verbal abuse. "People have been throwing some wild figures around," says Lieut. Col. James Cassella, a spokesman for the Defense Department. "My understanding is that it's kind of an apples and oranges comparison." But the military's method may actually underestimate the problem, since it long ignored violence against a legion of nonmarried partners, an especially important omission, considering that one recent study found that single men represent nearly 60 percent of soldiers using a gun or knife in attacks on women. And there is no way to corroborate independently the figures the military releases on domestic violence cases that are handled through military judicial processes, since they are shielded, as civilian police records are not, from public view. Moreover, the cited studies did take into account the most important demographic differences— the apples and oranges—in military and civilian populations.

Mary Beth Loucks-Sorrell, interim director of the North Carolina Coalition Against Domestic Violence, a statewide umbrella group based in Durham, is convinced that women partnered with soldiers face disproportionate risks of domestic abuse, a conclusion reached through years of fielding reports from abused women (and occasionally men). Just since [January 2002], she said, North Carolina's 100 counties have seen at least forty men kill their partners, seven of them in Cumberland County, where Fort Bragg is located. Reports of abuse from military communities are not only more frequent, but the level of violence they describe is more extreme and, according to domestic violence groups, has become worse over the past several years. Soldiers also terrorize their partners in unique ways, reminding the women of the sniper and bare-handed killing skills they acquire in training.

On hearing of the four murders, many people in the general public and media asked whether the soldiers might have suffered from post-combat trauma or simply, as the military suggested, from the stress of deployment and its disruption of family life. Some commentators on the right went so far as to suggest that these killings are another kind of war casualty and give us one more reason for gratitude to US soldiers. On the left, the combat-stress explanation can draw on the notion of the soldier as a victim of class violence and reluctant imperial tool. In both these views, the soldier's home-front violence is the traumatic outcome of "what he saw" in combat rather than the much more significant trauma of what he did.

Stan Goff, a Special Forces veteran of Vietnam and Haiti, and now a democracy activist in Raleigh, scoffs at the "TV docudrama version of war" underlying this assumption. "Go to Afghanistan," he says, "where you are insulated from outside scrutiny, and all the taboos you learned as a child are suspended. You take life more and more with impunity, and discover that the universe doesn't collapse when you drop the hammer on a human being, and for some, there is a real sense of power. For others, for all maybe, it's PTSD [post-traumatic stress disorder] on the installment plan." The effect of this sense of impunity was evident when a Special Forces soldier, who was once arrested for domestic violence, told one of us that Memorial Day ceremonies always left him pondering why he would get medals for killing others in battle but would be arrested if he killed his wife.

Examining the Effects of Drugs

A distracting sideshow to the murder investigations has been a UPI [United Press International] report suggesting the soldiers might have suffered side-effects of Lariam, a drug the Army gives prophylactically to troops going to malarial areas. Prescribed for 22 million people since 1985, Lariam use is associated with vivid dreams, insomnia and dizziness and is known to be correlated with neuropsychiatric problems in a tiny percentage of cases, found in one large study to be 1 in 13,000. (In the wake of Pentagon stonewalling on the health effects of anthrax inoculation and depleted uranium weapons, Defense Department denial that Lariam is a problem might justifiably be taken with a grain of salt, but the epidemiological numbers suggest that skepticism is warranted about the drug's relationship to domestic violence.) Nonetheless, the Pentagon has sent an epidemiological team to Fort Bragg to investigate this and other potential roots of the murders.

In the Pentagon's approach to the problem and in virtually all media accounts, gender has been left hidden in plain sight. As in the 1990s schoolyard shootings, where a rhetoric of "kids killing kids" disguised the fact that boys were overwhelmingly the killers, here the soldiers are seen simply as an occupational group and the problem, at most, as one of an institutional culture where soldiers have difficulty "asking for help" from family service providers abundantly available at installations like Bragg.

A Culture of Violence

Not only does the military remain by reputation the most "masculine" occupation available, but people in Fayetteville and in the armed forces generally consider Special Forces and Delta Force, where three of the four men worked, the Army's toughest units. Special Operations units are some of the last in the military to exclude women, and they also specialize in unconventional warfare, which is combat that often follows neither the letter nor the spirit of the rules of war. As a sign in a Special Forces training area says: "Rule #1. There are no rules. Rule #2. Follow Rule #1." Such a macho, above-the-law culture provides not a small part of the recipe for domestic violence. Combine this with a double standard of sexuality, one in which, as many soldiers and their wives told us, some couples expect infidelity to take place on Special Forces deployments—where the men operate with unusual autonomy and are often surrounded by desperately poor women—whereas the infidelity of wives, reactive or not, real or imagined, can be punished with violence.

If there was a common thread that tied the murdered women's lives together, it was the one identified by Tanya Biank, a *Fayetteville Observer* reporter: All four of them had expressed a desire to leave their marriages, a situation that domestic violence workers have identified as the most dangerous time for women in abusive relationships. For that is when the control these men tend to insist on in their relationships appears about to dissolve. Christine Hansen is executive director of the Connecticut-based Miles Foundation, which has assisted more than 7,000 victims of military-related violence since 1996. Military personnel, she says, are controlled from above at work even more than most US workers, and many come home looking to reassert control, often with violence. The anxieties about control, and consequently the violence, flare up most often before and after military deployments, Hansen says, as soldiers lose and then try to reinstate control. As the war in Afghanistan began [in] October [2001], for example, "We could literally tell what units were being deployed from where, based on the volume of calls we received from given bases. Then the same thing happened on the other end, when they came back."

After the wave of murders at Fort Bragg, the Senate set aside money for a new Pentagon investigation of military domestic violence—the latest in a long line of commissions established over the course of the many gendered scandals of the past ten years, from Tailhook to Aberdeen. Such investigations have neither stemmed the problem nor prompted the military to recognize the fundamental role of violent masculinity in crimes like the Fort Bragg killings. This would entail seeing the murders as a piece of the larger, epidemic problem of violent abuse by men within the military, including rape of female (and some male) soldiers and civilians, lesbian- and gay-bashing, and brutal hazing rituals, as Dorothy Mackey, director of Survivors Take Action Against Abuse by Military Personnel, a national network of counseling groups based in Ohio, points out.

Prosecuting Batterers

Of the 1,213 reported domestic violence incidents known to military police and judged to merit disciplinary action in 2000, the military could report only twenty-nine where the perpetrator was court-martialed or sent to a civilian court for prosecution. The military claims to have no data on the disciplinary outcome of the 12,068 cases reported to family services in that year. They also have no record of the outcome of 81 percent of the police cases. This poor record-keeping and apparent reluctance to prosecute offenders can be explained by the military's institutional interests in burying the problem of domestic violence. One such interest is public relations. To recruit and retain a force of 1.4 million, including women and married men, remains a monumental task that would only be made harder by widespread knowledge of the extent of the violence. Second, there are financial motives. Many soldiers cost more than $100,000 each to recruit and train, money that goes down the drain if a soldier is discharged or imprisoned. Finally, there is the continuing, if waning, power of a belief, still widespread in the prevolunteer and mostly unmarried force, that "if the Army had wanted you to have a wife, it would have issued you one." Protecting women from domestic violence in this environment falls even farther down the list of missions to be accomplished than it does in the civilian sector.

Obstacles to Escape

The difficulties women have in leaving their abusers are well-known. Military wives have additional disincentives. The unemployment rate for military wives is extremely high—hovering around 20 percent for those living at Fort Bragg—and those who do find employment are often stuck in the minimum-wage retail jobs that are the main work available in the satellite economy around most large posts. If they report abuse, they risk not only retribution from their husbands, as do women in the civilian world, but loss of their total family income, healthcare and other benefits, and even their housing and neighbors if their husband is discharged. One Army program does provide $900 a month plus healthcare for the few abused women whose husbands are removed from the force for domestic violence. Fort Bragg has no domestic violence shelter, though for many years was donating a paltry $10 a day to a local shelter when military wives fled there.

Women married to abusive soldiers have been calling the Fayette-ville newspaper and domestic violence shelters around the country in sharply higher numbers since the Fort Bragg killings were reported. According to advocates, many callers are terrified, fearing they will be next because of their partners' ongoing violence and death threats. Women have spoken out about the frequent failure of commanders to take their calls for help seriously. And they have complained that they were often sent to military chaplains, some of whom advised them that suffering is a woman's lot or that their husbands were just "working off some excess energy." One counselor at Fort Bragg was quoted in the *Washington Post* describing how she tells women to prepare their partners returning from deployment for changes they have made in his absence, like cutting their hair short: "He might be thinking about running his hands through that long, luxuriant hair," she said. "Don't surprise your husband." After the murders, rather than implementing new measures to protect the thousands of women already in its police and family advocacy files, in late August [2002] the military began to screen soldiers leaving Afghanistan for mental health problems. While this may not be a bad idea in general, it presumes that combat stress alone is what leads to domestic abuse, and creates the illusion that something is being done about domestic violence without addressing its fundamental causes.

The cultural celebration of soldiers, which has grown more fervent since the war on terror began, has hampered attempts to address the problem. In good times, critical views of military practice are not well received; in the new atmosphere of intimidation fostered by the Bush Administration since September 11 [2001], they may be considered tantamount to treason. Christine Hansen, who has received death threats since her foundation appeared in news stories about the murders, notes that some civilian judges have been even more reluctant than before to convict soldiers of domestic violence, when doing so would trigger the Lautenberg Amendment, a 1996 law that prohibits convicted abusers from owning firearms. The idea that the soldier makes an unrecompensable sacrifice creates a halo effect, so that the murderers are painted as victims of the horrors of combat, while scant attention is paid to the women they killed or the system's failure to prevent their deaths. As Stan Goff told us, soldiers in this climate can turn to their wives and say, "The culture's worshiping me. Why aren't you?"

In a widely disseminated Pentagon directive issued [in] November [2001], Deputy Defense Secretary Paul Wolfowitz declared that "domestic violence is an offense against the institutional values of the military." But domestic violence, rape and male supremacism itself are not anomalies or sideshows to war; instead, they lie near the center of how it is prosecuted and narrated. The millions of women throughout the world currently threatened by soldiers will look to their advocates and each other for their ultimate safety, and may have a unique appreciation for the ironies of focusing on more abstract terrors when they face such immediate dangers so close to home.

BATTERED WOMEN IN COMMUNITIES OF COLOR

Rinku Sen

Rinku Sen is the publisher of *ColorLines* magazine and the director of the New York office of the Applied Research Center, which conducts research on issues related to racial equity. In the following selection, Sen explores the unique problems that women of color face in dealing with domestic violence. For instance, she writes, African Americans are often hesitant to report cases of domestic violence because they do not want to contribute further to the high rate of incarceration of black men. Because many American Indian tribes function as sovereign nations, Sen explains, these communities are reluctant to involve outside authorities and instead try to develop their own programs for helping battered women. Immigrant women tend not to call the police because they fear that they will be deported, the author states. Sen asserts that current criminal justice strategies do not adequately address the needs of minority women who are battered, and she suggests alternatives to criminalization as the primary solution to domestic violence.

One out of four American women becomes a victim of domestic violence during her lifetime; one in three African American men comes under the supervision of the police and courts before the age of 25. Sometimes these two realities create conflicting loyalties, especially for women of color, who desperately need solutions to both problems.

Women of color have been involved in the battered women's movement since its beginnings. Yet sometimes communities of color display deep, race-based ambivalence about the causes of, and solutions to, domestic violence. In the O.J. Simpson case, the African American community's recognition of racism in the courts overrode concern about abuse (or murder?) of a privileged white woman. [In 1995, Simpson was acquitted in a criminal trial of the charge of murdering his ex-wife, Nicole Brown Simpson.]

In the early 1970s, the original leaders of the battered women's movement made a conscious, strategic decision to insist that batter-ing was universal, took place in all communities, and in all classes. Chuck Turner, a black counselor and manager at Emerge, which pro-vides rehabilitation services to court-supervised batterers of all races, identifies one of those commonalities: "that the batterer feels entitled to services and authority from women, and believes that if she is not behaving in the way that fits that role, he has the right to punish her." Focusing on the universality of domestic violence helped get woman battering on the national agenda.

In so doing, advocates of all colors avoided the view that men of color might be more likely to be violent toward their partners, or that women of color were more tolerant of violence against themselves or their peers. They feared that such views would play into preexisting racist stereotypes.

Increased Risk of Abuse?

Statistics from the National Family Violence Survey show that poverty puts women at added risk for sustaining physical and psychological injury. Since women and children of color constitute disproportionate numbers of the poor, it may be that domestic violence is more preva-lent in communities of color because of poverty.

However, many anti–domestic violence activists question the accu-racy of such statistics. Alana Bowman, who is white, is a deputy city attorney in Los Angeles and former supervisor of that county's domes-tic violence prosecution unit. She suggests that domestic violence might simply be more visible in poor, immigrant, and racial minority communities because "people call the police when they need any kind of social service because the police are there 24 hours a day and they are free." By contrast, some middle and upper class women, mostly white, can choose to hide their bruises and wounds by going to a private doctor instead of the emergency room, and can buy an airplane ticket to escape instead of going to a shelter.

Yet, many activists are convinced that domestic violence takes dis-tinctive forms in different communities of color. Long-time African American activist and researcher Beth Richie says that the search for solutions has to "recognize that women who are addicted to an illegal drug, or trying to live on subsistence wages, or have unclear immigra-tion status, experience violence differently because of our further marginalized position."

The Effectiveness of Criminal Justice Strategies

Activists express mixed feelings about the effectiveness of criminal jus-tice strategies to prevent and stop domestic violence, and in keeping women safe. Bowman and Turner support criminalization because domestic violence is legally defined as a serious crime that carries esca-lating sanctions. Bowman considers herself to be "in the business of making criminals out of men who do not see themselves as criminals," further noting that eighty percent of the men who batter women have no other contact with the criminal justice system. Though distressed by the racist criminalization of African American men, Richie acknowledges that many women's lives have been saved by police intervention.

None of those interviewed for this article believe criminal prosecution alone is adequate to deal with the root causes of violence against women. Richie argues that criminalization does little to raise consciousness or protect individual women in black communities. Oliver Williams, director of the National Institute on Domestic Violence in the African American Community, says that the criminal justice system can only "capture the easy targets—low-income white men and men of color. We can't expect the legal system to catch all the people doing the battering, so there have to be community sanctions for batterers and community protection for women."

Unfortunately, criminalizing domestic violence ensures that some women, mostly of color, get no help. Many women of color simply will not call the police for fear of what will happen to themselves or their abusive partner in the hands of law enforcement officers. Many immigrant women will not call for fear of having their immigration status questioned. Mandatory arrest laws are often used by police to arrest both partners in a dispute, with the claim that both partners were being violent. Sue Osthoff, a white woman who directs the National Clearinghouse for the Defense of Battered Women, says that "if we keep increasing criminal sanctions, we will increasingly see that who is getting pulled into that net are women, especially women of color."

Some groups are pursuing alternatives to criminalization that focus on raising awareness and censuring batterers. Sakhi, a group of South Asian women in New York, regularly conducts marches and rallies, sometimes at the homes of batterers. Leah Aldridge, an African American who works at the Los Angeles Commission on Assaults Against Women, runs a program to reeducate teens about rape and battering. Working through schools and community organizations, this program aims to break the cycle in which children experience family violence and go on to either tolerate it or perpetrate it as adults.

Domestic Violence in Native American Communities

In Indian country, anti–domestic violence activists confront the benefits and costs of criminal justice and shelter systems from a position of sovereignty. Charen Artichoker, an Oglala Lakota and Hochunk woman who directs Cangleska, Inc., in Rapid City, South Dakota, says that communities that operate a sovereign tribal force "recognize the police as front-line people who come and help whether you have a domestic dispute or need your refrigerator moved." She says tribal control of the police force makes a tremendous difference "because it is our own system and the cops are Indian."

On the other hand, Artichoker points out the racist history of Bureau of Indian Affairs' policing in Indian country. Additionally, many Indians choose not to call the authorities in cases of rape, severe violence, or murder because such crimes would be handled by the Federal Bureau of Investigation. Activist Maggie Escovita Steele (Chiricahua Apache) says "they take forever to come, and nothing's going to happen." Artichoker, who supports criminalization in general, says that calling the Feds "is not the stance of a sovereign nation."

Such cases force many Indian communities to develop their own sanctions against abusers, sanctions which can be politically delicate in small communities where everybody knows one another. Escovita Steele recounts an example in which a young woman was killed, splitting the community over family and friendship loyalties. The young people of the community got together, called out the perpetrators, asked the tribe not to pay their legal fees, and to pay all the burial costs for the victim. Such interventions require high levels of consciousness by advocates who, Artichoker says, push communities to "get past the stigma about ratting each other out."

Artichoker's organization has developed a shelter system that supports abused women. "We've built our shelter to be different from the usual. We don't keep the food, phones, or people locked up, and have no curfew." Although the shelter helps, Artichoker wants an Indian-run criminal justice system which would pull the batterer, not the woman, out of the home and community. "I wish we had a place where the men would have to stay, but where they'd get some information about how to change their behavior. Right now all he gets is the guys saying 'forget the bitch, have another beer.'"

The Challenge of Dealing with Domestic Violence

While many anti–domestic violence activists have pushed for public awareness to help prevent violence, others question whether batterer re-education programs get to the root causes of violence any more effectively than criminalization has. Bowman feels that much of the new money entering the field is going to questionable programs which promote individual rather than social solutions. Such campaigns threaten perpetrators with jail, but fail to counter men's sense of entitlement to control women's lives through the use of intimidation and violence. Turner admits that "programs like ours have some benefits, but their effectiveness depends on the attitudes of the community surrounding the couple. Attitudes that blame the woman or deny the abuse create a framework that gives men a lot of room to deny their own responsibility."

Women of color also wonder whether they can expect support from white battered women's activists to specifically address domestic violence in communities of color. Richie says women of color increasingly feel able to act without support from white women, but that white activists are also increasingly open to questioning criminalization as the main solution to domestic violence. She thinks some of this openness stems from white women's negative experiences with criminalization—being hassled by the cops, getting arrested themselves, going to prison for killing their abusers, losing time from work and school while trying to prosecute abusers, or suffering from declining economic status that makes leaving less of an option.

Still, Richie questions whether the anti–domestic violence movement's internal critics, including herself, will be able to "undo our rigid stance about [the universality of battering and the need to sanction batterers] without demeaning the integrity of our own work over the last 30 years."

In short, women of color are between a rock and a hard place: perhaps at greater risk for domestic violence than white women because of poverty (of self and of partner); unable to trust the police for themselves or their partners; less able to rely on internal community resources because of low awareness of domestic violence; and confronted with reluctance from progressive people of all colors to further criminalize men of color.

Violence in Teenage Relationships

Samantha Levine

In the following selection, Samantha Levine discusses the incidence of battering experienced by adolescent girls in their romantic relationships. According to Levine, the problem of violence in teenage relationships is widespread; she cites a study released in 2001 that found that nearly one in five teenage girls had been physically or sexually abused by a date. Boys who witness domestic violence in their homes are much more likely to become abusive toward their romantic partners, she reports. Teenage girls may misinterpret the abuse as an intense form of caring, Levine states, or they may tolerate the abuse in order to maintain the relationship. Furthermore, the author explains, girls who are battered by their boyfriends run an increased risk of engaging in negative or dangerous behaviors, including drug use, unsafe sex, eating disorders, and suicide attempts. Levine is a journalist with *U.S. News & World Report*.

Michael was so gorgeous. Tall, with dark hair and deep brown eyes—all the girls agreed he was hot. So when he asked Kristen out, she was thrilled. She was 14, he was a year older. They dated for a few months, then two years later, as high school freshmen near Boston, they rekindled the relationship.

"Everything was great," says Kristen, "for about a month." Then one day Michael got annoyed with her for being a few minutes late to meet him. Without warning, he backhanded her across the face. He immediately apologized, and she made him vow he would never hit her again. He promised. "Then it just got worse," she says. "Right then, I should've told somebody and got help. But I didn't."

Kristen's nightmarish experience would seem like an unfortunate anomaly if it weren't for the fact that versions of it happen all the time. A startling new report published [in 2001] in the *Journal of the American Medical Association* reveals that nearly 1 in 5 girls surveyed had been physically or sexually abused by a date. The first large-scale report on violence within teenage intimate relationships, it shows that these young women are also more likely to abuse drugs and alcohol, engage in risky sexual behavior, get pregnant, adopt unhealthful eating practices, and attempt suicide. Perhaps even more disturbing, it correlates with anecdotal reports that suggest violence—from black eyes and fat lips to broken bones and rape—is a normal part of the dating ritual for a significant number of adolescents.

Dating Violence Is a Widespread Problem

Though the study looks only at public school girls who live in Massachusetts—using that state's version of the biannual federal Youth Risk Behavior Survey—the authors say these disturbing results have nationwide significance. "The exact numbers may differ slightly from state to state, but this is a problem that is affecting very large numbers of girls," says the study's lead researcher, Jay G. Silverman, director of violence prevention programs at the Harvard School of Public Health. It doesn't shock those who work with abused teens. "We are experiencing this on a daily basis," says Anne Canny Wargo of the Massachusetts outreach group Help for Abused Women and their Children (HAWC). "Having this study gives credibility to what we are doing."

When asked if they have been shoved, slapped, hit, or forced into a sexual act by a date, an average of 9.5 percent of the 4,163 girls surveyed in 1997 and 1999 reported physical abuse. Nearly 4 percent reported sexual abuse and 6 percent reported both. Deeper analysis of the questionnaires revealed that abused girls were eight to nine times more likely to have attempted suicide, four to six times more likely to have ever been pregnant, three to five times more likely to have ever used cocaine, and three to four times more likely to have used unhealthful dieting methods such as laxatives or vomiting. In some cases, the pervasive fear and intimidation in abusive relationships deter girls from asking partners to use condoms or other contraception, thus upping their risk of pregnancy, Silverman says. And abuse can exacerbate depression, a leading factor in suicide.

Why are so many girls in these relationships? For that answer, experts say, look to the boys who abuse them: The correlation between boys who witness domestic violence in their homes and later become batterers themselves is much stronger, Silverman says, than the link between girls who see violence and then become victims. Young men also may believe masculinity means physical aggression and fear that acting attentive and supportive toward women will win them disrespect from their peers. Girls may think solving problems in relationships means tolerating abuse, or may interpret the abuse as just very intense caring. Still others may feel they have nowhere to turn for help.

In addition to the need for more research into the dangerous paths taken by abused girls, Silverman says there must be greater understanding of the reasoning of boys who batter as well as intervention to prevent violence. "Young women are not bringing this problem on themselves," he says. "There is a historical entitlement of boys and men to control the behavior of their female partners, and we are dealing with that legacy. We need to be working now with youth. We can't wait."

CHAPTER 2

BATTERED WOMEN AND THE LAW

IMPROVEMENTS IN THE LEGAL RESPONSE TO DOMESTIC VIOLENCE

Cara Feinberg

In the following selection, Cara Feinberg describes recent advances in the way that domestic violence cases are handled by the legal system. According to Feinberg, these changes have largely arisen from the work of feminist advocates, who first drew attention to domestic violence as a legitimate social problem. In particular, she highlights the passage in 1994 of the Violence Against Women Act, the first federal law to address the issue of domestic abuse. The act mandates a variety of approaches toward preventing and solving the problem of violence against women, including special training for federal and state judges. In addition, the author observes, many state and local law enforcement departments have made significant progress in their treatment of accused batterers and their victims. However, Feinberg concludes, much room for improvement remains, particularly in areas of the country where awareness about domestic violence is still limited. Feinberg is the assistant editor of the *American Prospect*, a liberal political magazine. She also writes the "World Responds" column for the *American Prospect Online*.

As late as the 1960s, if you looked at American newspapers, police reports, medical records, and legal texts, you would find little mention of domestic violence anywhere. "In the last few decades, there has been a great surge in attention to this issue," says Clare Dalton, Northeastern University's Matthews Distinguished University Professor of Law, who is a leading feminist legal scholar and a pioneer in the development of legal education about domestic violence. A founder of Northeastern's domestic-violence clinical program and the Domestic Violence Institute (an interdisciplinary educational, research, and service organization), Dalton served as a consultant on [documentary filmmaker Frederick] Wiseman's film [about domestic violence] and led discussions about the issue at several showings of *Domestic Violence* in the Boston area.

Cara Feinberg, "Hitting Home," *American Prospect*, vol. 13, April 8, 2002, p. 30. Copyright © 2002 by The American Prospect, Inc., 5 Broad Street, Boston, MA 02109. All rights reserved. Reproduced by permission.

The Violence Against Women Act

"Right up into the 1980s, we still had states in the Union with out-of-date immunity laws based on common law from the 1800s, protecting men who beat their wives," Dalton says. "It was only 10 years ago now that the Supreme Court was even ready to recognize the severity of domestic violence in our country—only eight years ago that Congress addressed it on a federal level with the Violence Against Women Act [VAWA]."

That legislation, passed initially in 1994 and renewed by Congress in 2000, was a milestone: It was the first federal law ever to address the issue, and it came at the problem with a variety of solutions, including funding for women's shelters, a national domestic-abuse hot line, rape education-and-prevention programs, training for federal and state judges, new remedies for battered immigrants, and criminal enforcement of interstate orders of protection.

Feminism and Legal Reform

As Dalton points out, VAWA would have been impossible without the work that began with the feminist movement of the 1960s and 1970s. "Our latest campaign against domestic violence grew directly out of the movement," she says. "For the first time, women were getting together and talking about their experiences and discovering the great prevalence of these unspoken terrors. Emerging feminist theory allowed women to connect with each other and to the ideas that feminists had been arguing for all along: that women's legally sanctioned subordination within the family was denying them equality."

Taking their cue from the civil-rights and antiwar movements earlier, feminist activists began to see the law not only as an important tool for protecting victims but as a way to define domestic violence as a legitimate social problem. Local legal groups and grass-roots advocacy organizations began to develop legal remedies based on the link between sexual discrimination and violence. Starting in the sixties, lawyers began to seek civil-protective or restraining orders to keep batterers away from their victims. Courts began to create special rules for domestic-violence cases and custody cases involving children from violent homes. And by the mid-1990s, Congress had passed VAWA. Today, feminist advocates for battered women have begun to draw important interconnections among battering, poverty, welfare reform, homelessness, immigration, employment, gun control, and many other areas of concern. They are working with all sorts of organizations to step up education and reform. . . .

Police Response

According to Elizabeth M. Schneider, a professor at Brooklyn Law School and the author of *Battered Women and Feminist Lawmaking* (2000), one of the first and most important legal issues to come to the attention of the feminist movement in the 1960s was the failure of police to protect battered women from assault. By the 1970s, class-action lawsuits were filed in New York City and Oakland, California. All of a sudden, domestic violence was considered a crime against the public and the state, not just the individual.

Yet even these victories and others like them initially made little headway in police attitudes and practices. [In 1983], a woman named Tracey Thurman was nearly beaten to death in Torrington, Connecticut, before the police came to her aid. Though Thurman had reported her estranged husband's threats and harassment to the police repeatedly for over a year, it wasn't until she called in utter desperation, fearing for her life, that the police responded. They sent only one officer, however, who arrived 25 minutes after the call was placed, pulled up across the street from Thurman's house, and sat in his car while Thurman's husband chased her across the yard, slashed her with a knife, stabbed her in the neck, knocked her to the ground, and then stabbed her 12 more times.

Permanently disfigured, Tracey Thurman brought what became a landmark case to the Supreme Court, which found that the city police had violated her 14th Amendment right to "equal protection of the laws" and awarded her $2.3 million in compensatory damages. Almost immediately, the State of Connecticut adopted a new, comprehensive domestic-violence law calling for the arrest of assaultive spouses. In the year after the measure took effect, the number of arrests for domestic assault increased 92 percent, from 12,400 to 23,830.

Problems Remain Widespread

"We'd all like to look at our progress and be optimistic," says Clare Dalton. "But if you look at the most recent statistics from the Justice Department, the number of women dying in domestic-violence situations hasn't changed. The problem is as widespread as ever.

"But there is one interesting thing here," Dalton notes. "While the number of deaths among women hasn't changed, fatalities among men have dropped significantly. This, in truth, is our first real triumph. If women feel they can get help—if they believe the police will come when they call them, if they understand they will get support and have a place to go where they will be safe with their children— then fewer are pushed to the wall. Fewer will resort to killing or dying at the hand of their abuser."

The Tampa Example

Such wisdom has not been lost on the City of Tampa Police Department, whose progressive, community-wide response to the problem Frederick Wiseman chose to film for *Domestic Violence*. Tampa's network of coordinated, cooperative services—from law enforcement, to

social services, to the legal system—is a model example of similar programs around the country.

"We now have a zero-tolerance policy toward domestic violence
here in Tampa," said Lieutenant Rod Reder, a 24-year veteran of the
Hillsborough County Sheriff's Office in Tampa, when reached by
phone. A former supervisor for the Sex Crimes Division and one-time
member of the Governor's Domestic and Sexual Violence Task Force,
Reder is now widely considered to be an expert in the field of domestic and sexual violence. Under the auspices of the U.S. Department of
Justice, he runs training sessions for law-enforcement officers at con-
ferences nationwide. "We discovered there were so many simple
things we weren't doing . . . to help victims of domestic violence,"
Reder said. "And we found there really is only one way to make things
work. All the community players have to come to the table; otherwise, it's the victim's safety that gets compromised."

The catalyst for Tampa's adoption of community cooperation was a
woman named Mabel Bexley, who in 1981 pushed Reder to bring
police practices in line with new domestic-violence laws, and who two
years later became the director of a women's shelter called the Spring.
In her 19-year tenure there, Bexley, now 65 and recently retired,
expanded the Spring—which is the focus of much of Wiseman's documentary—from a three-bedroom house with more than a dozen
women and children huddled inside to a 102-bed facility with 120
employees and a $4-million budget.

A Zero-Tolerance Campaign

Reder and Bexley teamed up again in 1995, when Tampa hit an all-
time high in domestic-violence–related homicide, to work alongside
members of the state attorney's office and the 13th Judicial Circuit
Court to form the zero-tolerance campaign against domestic abuse.
Reder and the Hillsborough County police then formed a special
domestic-violence unit and developed a three-day training seminar
for all seven local law-enforcement agencies.

"We do all sorts of things now to make the system work," said
Reder. "When police answer a domestic-violence call, they are required to file a report—even if there is no arrest—just so the incident
is documented. We had deputies who would walk away from incidents saying, 'No harm, no foul,' and would leave with no report," he
recalled. "But now officers are required to document domestics by
state law. You start dinging a few deputies and taking disciplinary
action, and word gets out real quick: If you go to a domestic, write a
report."

According to Reder, Tampa officers have also become very aggressive about arrests: "We used to think we were doing the right thing by
not arresting the man—we didn't want to get him any angrier than he
already was. In the past, many officers looked at domestic-violence

calls as a waste of time or a private family matter. Now we consider them some of the most dangerous calls there are."

Addressing Gaps in the System

Hillsborough County has also addressed other gaps in the system. "We've sent advocates to go pick up victims at their homes so they'd be sure to get to court," said Reder. "We used to have communal waiting rooms in the courthouse, but now we have separate ones so victims won't have to face their abusers before their trial begins. To file an injunction, you used to have to fill out a complicated 25-page form that was only available in English. This alone used to scare people away, so now we have bilingual advocates and lawyers available to help people fill them out."

This is where the Spring comes in. Though most victims who arrive at the shelter are running for their lives and have no desire even to consider legal action against their abusers at that point, the facility employs an on-site attorney to help them navigate the judicial system and pursue the available options. In addition, each one of the Spring's hot-line operators is a deputy of the court who can file injunctions at any hour of the day or night. This is crucial, because the most dangerous time for abuse victims actually begins the moment they choose to leave their homes. "The Bureau of Justice statistics say that one-third of all women murdered in the U.S. are killed by an intimate," says Jennifer Dunbar, who works at the Spring. "But of those 30 percent, 65 percent are murdered when they leave. It's our job to make sure [victims are] protected at this point."

Coordinating Services

Nearly 40 years after the first feminist activists in the women's movement brought domestic violence to the nation's attention, the policies have largely been set and the laws are finally on the books. Now it's a question of making sure that the systems work and helping the larger community to understand, recognize, and accommodate the needs of battered women. "Right now, we're working on expanding efforts into other systems, like job placement, affordable housing, welfare reform, and child-protective services," says Lynn Rosenthal of the [Washington, D.C.–based National Network to End Domestic Violence]. "A number of states now have special domestic-violence provisions within their welfare systems and housing programs. For instance, under the original job-placement programs in the TANF [Temporary Assistance for Needy Families] program, people who showed up tardy three times to the program would lose their benefits. A battered woman might have tremendous problems meeting these criteria—her husband could still be sabotaging her efforts." Rosenthal adds: "It's easy to see how our own well-intended programs could send her right back to her batterer."

Throughout the country, states have begun to integrate their systems and have developed new, progressive programs to deal with domestic violence. Though they vary in their specific reforms, many have expanded their legal definition of domestic violence to include nonmarried and nontraditional couples. And some, shifting their focus from punishment to rehabilitation, have begun to examine the root causes of violence in the first place. Programs like EMERGE in Cambridge, Massachusetts, work with batterers to find nonviolent ways to express their anger; many others educate children and teens—ideally, before any battering starts. A number of states have created specialized domestic-violence courts so that the judges hearing these cases are not only familiar with and sympathetic to the special circumstances surrounding battering cases but can follow them from start to finish.

A Long Way to Go

Yet for all the progress that has been made in addressing domestic violence, Wiseman's film makes clear that there is a long way yet to go. One problem is how practically and psychologically difficult it can be for a victim to leave her batterer. But another is the complexity of the political environment itself. As elected officials come and go, their varying agendas affect the winds of legislative change and shift fiscal priorities along with idealistic convictions. According to Robin Thompson, the former executive director of the Florida Governor's Task Force on Domestic Violence, in order for a state to stay vigilant in its fight against domestic abuse there must be "a bedrock of political commitment"—be it a designated task force or a group of grass-roots activists invested in educating and uniting their community. Awareness alone is not enough.

And while states may have implemented great judicial and law-enforcement reforms, if these are not closely monitored and coordinated, they can still fall short of their goals. For instance, if an accused batterer is arrested right away but then must wait six months for a trial, the victim is still largely unprotected. Or if a judge orders a defendant to participate in an intervention program but no one checks to see if he complies, the sentence may be useless.

Obstacles to reform certainly don't fall neatly along partisan lines. A liberal judge might opt for a surprisingly lenient sentence for a defendant, while a conservative judge might make an equally counterintuitive ruling, viewing the court as the woman's traditional protectorate. Yet in communities where awareness of partner abuse remains limited—and partisan issues such as welfare, gun ownership, and "family values" remain entwined with domestic violence—reform movements lag well behind their counterparts in more progressive places.

A QUESTION OF CUSTODY: CHILD PROTECTION AGENCIES VERSUS BATTERED WOMEN

Chris Lombardi

Battered women who report their abuse face the possibility of having their children removed from their custody by child protective services, Chris Lombardi writes in the following selection. According to Lombardi, for years domestic violence advocates have stressed that children are detrimentally affected by living in a household where their mother is being physically abused, even when the children themselves are not being beaten. These advocates hoped this argument would prompt child welfare institutions to intervene in such situations to help both the mother and her children, the author states. Instead, she explains, in some cases child protection agencies have accused battered women of harming their children by exposing them to an environment of domestic violence. Lombardi specifically focuses on New York's Administration for Children's Services, which has placed the children of battered women in foster homes after charging their mothers with "engaging in domestic violence." Based in New York, Lombardi is a freelance journalist and a women's advocate who works for issues of social justice.

When Sharwline Nicholson thinks about what happened in January 1999, it's not about the fact that her boyfriend beat her for the first and last time. Instead she thinks about her children, who were removed that night and put into foster care, while Nicholson was charged with child neglect—for an offense called "engaging in domestic violence." "I've had no time for knowing I was a victim of domestic violence," Sharwline (pronounced like "Charlene") Nicholson says. "When they removed my children, the physical pain was overlooked."

As the lead plaintiff in a federal lawsuit against the City and State of New York, Nicholson's now part of a landmark decision—rendered

Chris Lombardi, "Justice for Battered Women," *Nation*, vol. 275, July 15, 2002, p. 24. Copyright © 2002 by The Nation magazine/The Nation Company, Inc. Reproduced by permission.

in March 2001 by District Court Judge Jack Weinstein—that could change child welfare as we know it.

A Jamaican immigrant and single mother who works full time and attends college at night, Nicholson lives in Brooklyn with her son, Kendell, and baby daughter, Destinee. Destinee's father, Claude Barnett, had already moved to South Carolina, visiting "once a month or so to see the baby," Nicholson says. That day in January, Claude, who had never hit her before, broke her arm and smashed her face while Kendell was in school and the baby was asleep in the next room. He left before the police arrived, and Nicholson found a trusted neighbor to take care of her kids until she came home from the hospital.

In the hospital the next morning, she received her first call from the Administration for Children's Services (ACS), telling her they had removed her children, and ordering her to a Family Court hearing. By the time the court date arrived, the children were in foster care. She faced the bizarre charge of "engaging in domestic violence" without a lawyer: Only afterward was she assigned a series of overworked, underpaid Family Court lawyers, who had no time to do more than glance at her files.

It took three weeks for Nicholson to get her children back, during which time Kendell reported being hit by one foster parent and had asked the next, "Are you going to hit me?" And the neglect petition remained until Nicholson found help at Sanctuary for Families, a New York City social services provider for mothers and children affected by domestic violence. "At first, I couldn't believe what I was hearing," says Jill Zuccardy, director of the child protection project at Sanctuary. "Then more and more women were coming to me with the same set of experiences."

Like April Rodriguez, who sought refuge from her abusive husband at her grandmother's home: ACS followed her there and removed the kids because they didn't like the bedding provided. Or Ekaete Udoh, who'd finally obtained an order of protection after twenty years of abuse, after which her batterer returned to his native Nigeria; Udoh also faced a neglect petition for "engaging in domestic violence," while ACS placed her teenage daughters in foster care. Another woman, who actually asked ACS to help her with her alcoholic, abusing husband, was referred instead to family counseling and told to go to a shelter; when her husband threatened to kill her, ACS did nothing to help her but removed the children. Michele Garcia lost her children because she'd "blatantly refused to cooperate with ACS," since she insisted they only visit when previously agreed—fearing that unannounced visits would scare the children. (In Garcia's case, ACS ignored the advice of its own child protective services supervisor, Cheryl Meyers, who saw no reason for removal.)

All these removals occurred without the court orders required by ACS's own regulations except in an emergency. And all of these mothers found their way to Sanctuary, which filed a class-action lawsuit in January 2001 charging violation of both mothers' and children's civil rights.

Legal Recourse for Battered Women

The case was assigned to Judge Weinstein, who is famous for crafting remedies in cases involving Agent Orange, tobacco and asbestos, and has inserted his voice into debates on the death penalty and the Rockefeller drug laws. "He was unlike any judge I've encountered," says Nicholson. "He really wanted to be educated. He didn't want any half-and-half stories."

After a two-month trial that included forty-four witnesses, including Nicholson, nine other mothers in similar situations and numerous experts, Weinstein issued a landmark ruling on March 11 in the case, *In Re Nicholson, et al.* He found that ACS often alleges neglect by battered mothers simply for being battered; has failed to assist these mothers and to hold abusers accountable; has removed children unnecessarily; hasn't offered adequate training about domestic violence; and has promoted this bad behavior in its written policies. All of this, he explained in a 188-page, carefully worded decision, violates half the Bill of Rights. He cited the Fourth Amendment, the Ninth and even the Thirteenth, comparing the mothers' stigmatization and loss of control to slavery. He was perhaps most outraged by ACS's trashing of the Fourteenth Amendment, in its flagrant disrespect for due process.

Nicholson was awarded $150,000, with the other mothers receiving similar amounts; but the real weight of the judge's ruling is in his plan for change. Weinstein ordered ACS to stop removing children from mothers whose only "crime" is being battered, and to work collaboratively with domestic violence advocates to improve its approach to such cases. He also demanded that New York State more than double the compensation for publicly funded Family Court attorneys, so that these mothers can have the representation they deserve.

No one's addressed these issues in court before, and the national implications are huge. The only way to grasp the significance of the challenge Weinstein has thrown down is to look at the systems that have bred these abuses.

In Re Nicholson is about race and class as well as gender. Domestic violence crosses class barriers, but child protective agencies largely leave affluent families alone. Eighty-five percent of foster children in New York and the majority of the Nicholson plaintiffs are from black, Hispanic and immigrant families.

Domestic Violence and Child Abuse

How much does child maltreatment actually coexist with adult domestic violence? Published estimates range from 6.5 to 97 percent of child cases, though most advocates weigh in at 40–60 percent. Sharwline Nicholson, who's been talking to many women with children in the system, believes domestic violence is nearly always a factor in removal, even if the children are removed for drug use or genuine neglect: "Domestic violence is embedded. It's in there somewhere."

One might assume, then, that workers in child protection agencies are trained often and deeply in the dynamics of domestic violence, so as better to serve such families. But until recently, many child protective agencies saw battered women—and their advocates—as the enemy.

New York City's ACS was created after the 1995 death of Elisa Izquierdo, who was killed by her battered, crack-addicted mother despite positive assessments by what was then the Child Welfare Administration. In January 1996 the new agency, with Nicholas Scoppetta at its head, promised a new era for children. One of its operating principles was that "any ambiguity regarding the safety of the child will be resolved in favor of removing the child from harm's way." The agency drilled this mandate into the heads of ACS's frontline workers—most of whom are in their early 20s and arrive at their positions with a BA and less than a year's training—and told them they need a court order to remove children except in cases of "imminent danger." But that last phrase has allowed them the discretion to remove children without checking in with a judge, a domestic violence expert or even a supervisor.

When Nicholson was battered that winter night, they could have asked her where Barnett lived, if he had keys to the house (he didn't) and what she needed to stay safe. They could have helped Nicholson file a protective order against Barnett, or done it themselves on behalf of the children. But none of this was done. No one even listened, a few weeks later, when she told her caseworker that she hadn't been able to get an order since she didn't know his address. They ignored the fact that Barnett wasn't coming back and insisted that Nicholson agree not to go to the only home she had. Her children were leverage to get her to agree to their prescriptions. In Weinstein's courtroom, child protection manager Nat Williams testified that he'd kept the children from Nicholson in the hope that "once she got before the judge, that the judge would order her to cooperate."

Strict Policies Punish Victims

In many ways, the pattern of abuse by ACS and other child protective agencies is a sign of a campaign that backfired. "Domestic violence advocates have been saying for twenty years, what about the children?" says Alexandria Ruden, staff attorney at the Legal Aid Society of Cleveland and one of the authors of the Ohio Domestic Violence Law. Numerous academic studies, education campaigns and trainings have emphasized the idea that domestic violence has a detrimental effect on children living in the household. The hope, of course, was to get child-focused legislators and bureaucrats to take the issue seriously, and perhaps to enlist the powerful child-welfare apparatus on behalf of the woman, to protect the entire family from violence. The intent was not to generate a punitive response by the very institutions set up to provide assistance.

These campaigns were heard, all right—but in a way that abuses battered mothers instead of helping them. "In a way, these folks are doing what we told them," says Ruden.

Child protective workers have over and over again focused on what the mother should be doing, and responded punitively if she did not meet their expectations, instead of targeting the batterer. In Florida, after 6-year-old Kayla McKean was beaten to death in 1998, the state legislature passed one of the twenty-three "child witness" laws in this country. As a result of "Kayla's law," when an order of protection is filed, judges commonly notify the Department of Children and Family Services. This could have prompted any manner of creative solutions; by the time the law passed, there was an extensive shelter network and a great deal of expertise in response to domestic violence available to the department. Instead, there are numerous reports of child protective workers saying to mothers, "If you don't go to the shelter, we'll take your kids," according to Robin Hassler Thompson, of the Florida Coalition Against Domestic Violence, who said she was thrilled to hear of the Weinstein decision. "I said to myself, there are parallels here."

The same sentiment was echoed in Ohio by Ruden, who has already given copies of the decision to the Ohio Department of Children and Family Services, which was already in the process of developing a protocol on domestic violence.

"Judge Weinstein underscored the basic constitutional principles behind this suit," says Lois Weithorn, professor at Hastings Law School, whose article "Protecting Children From Exposure to Domestic Violence: The Use and Abuse of Child Maltreatment Statutes" was published in the November 2001 issue of the *Hastings Law Journal*. "The Supreme Court has stated over and over again that parents have the right to their children without government interference, unless it's absolutely necessary. Weinstein showed that reflexively removing children from the non-violent parent is a violation, and that ACS had not shown it to be necessary."

Prescription for Change

These advocates are also hailing Weinstein's section on "best practices," where the judge outlines clearly and thoughtfully what he thinks the agency should be doing instead. Drawing on experts such as Jeff Edleson and other authors of what's known in the field as the "Green Book," a publication of the National Council of Juvenile and Family Court Judges, he directs ACS to operate on the principle that the best way to protect the child is to protect the mother—which is to hold the batterer accountable while offering the mother the constellation of services she needs, from housing to job training to childcare. All of the above, of course, require help from myriad agencies, from police to school systems.

Weinstein's orders to ACS—that separation of battered mothers and their children should be an alternative of last resort, only after the agency has acted to protect mothers; that agency employees need to be trained in domestic violence; and that frontline caseworkers need clear guidance on the issues—are not simply suggestions. They have the force of law.

Since the lawsuit was filed, ACS has issued memorandums barring the use of the term "engaging in domestic violence," begun consulting with national domestic violence experts and increased by a few days the amount of domestic violence training mandated for frontline workers.

Still, ACS is now appealing the case to the Second Circuit Court of Appeals, citing a handful of state studies (challenged by Zuccardy in court) that suggest there were fewer illegal removals than Weinstein claimed. "They don't get it," says Jill Zuccardy of Sanctuary. "To prove constitutional violations, you only need one case. And we have so many more than one."

Weinstein granted a six-month stay in December 2001 in order to give ACS a chance to put an end to the constitutional offenses voluntarily by accelerating the domestic violence initiatives already in place. On June 20, 2002, as the stay expired, Weinstein refused a request to extend it for another three months, pending a possible settlement. He read aloud bits of ACS's monthly reports, finding "no indication . . . that anything has been done except with respect to talk about" change. . . .

As Weinstein pointed out, ACS needs to go back to the future: In 1993 the agency's "Zone C Project," in a target area in Manhattan, screened all child welfare cases for domestic violence and teamed caseworkers with domestic violence experts. The number of removals dropped dramatically. But before this program could be replicated, Elisa Izquierdo's death transformed the culture of the organization.

It was six years before they tried again in Manhattan's "Zone A," where the program had the benefit of more experience and coordination with police. Weinstein noted, "The batterer was arrested in 50 percent of the cases—a considerable increase—and an order of protection was provided to the victim in 42 percent of cases—also a large relative increase. The need for removals dropped dramatically; protective removals occurred in only 3 percent of cases—a substantial decrease." Yet the project was allowed to die, its practices incorporated only very slowly into ACS's new protocols and the "clinical consultation teams" they [established] in 2002.

Help for Child Protective Agencies

Other states have recognized the limits of what child protective agencies can do alone, with Minnesota modifying a strict "child witness" law that flooded its foster care system and Alaska pulling in all agencies to work on the problem together. It's promising that ACS is now consulting the Family Violence Prevention Fund, a national model in which domestic violence experts routinely train caseworkers and serve as a resource for battered women who enter the system. They might also look to the six Green Book demonstration projects across the country, such as San Jose's Domestic Violence Council, or to Judge Cindy Lederman's Dependency Court Intervention Project in Miami, which re-envisions how a family court can help.

All these solutions are expensive, at least at first, especially if you include the supportive resources battered women desperately need. But advocates point out that foster care is expensive too, let alone the long-term costs of incarceration as traumatized children grow into frustrated adults.

While ACS is happy to report its new initiatives, what's still unclear is whether the changes will penetrate to the frontlines. The core question for the agency: How high a percentage of its $2.1 billion budget is it willing to spend training frontline workers, and how much clout is it willing to give in-house domestic violence experts? Meanwhile, will New York State finally address the compensation of Family Court attorneys, currently the second lowest in the country?

Weinstein has now set the bar high for giving poor families in this country simple justice. The hope is that despite the turf battles large and small, the political will to implement these solutions will be found.

THE LEGAL STATUS OF BATTERED IMMIGRANT WOMEN

Lydia Brashear Tiede

Lydia Brashear Tiede is a lawyer in San Diego, California, who represents battered immigrant women and asylum seekers. In the following selection, she addresses the legal problems faced by battered immigrant women, including those who entered the United States illegally or without proper documentation. Tiede also examines the legal status of women who flee their home countries because of domestic violence. Once in the United States, these women are eligible to seek political asylum by establishing that they are the victims of gender-based persecution. However, the author argues, because of the stringent requirements of U.S. immigration law, such refugees often have a difficult time proving in court that they are part of a persecuted group and are therefore denied asylum. The legal system should provide protection for victims of domestic violence regardless of where the abuse occurs, Tiede concludes.

Domestic violence victims suffer unspeakable horrors at the hands of their abusers throughout the world. Two often-overlooked groups of domestic violence victims are women who are abused in their home countries and seek to immigrate to the United States and immigrant women living in the United States who are abused in this country. How the circumstances of the abuse are interpreted as well as how the available legal standards are applied in these cases depend exclusively on whether the victim is fleeing domestic violence that occurred in her home country or domestic violence occurring within the United States. Immigration law deals with these two groups of women separately. Each group must fulfill different legal requirements and evidentiary burdens.

Abuse Is Abuse

Women subjected to domestic violence in their home countries confront social, familial, and legal systems that refuse to acknowledge the

Lydia Brashear Tiede, "Battered Immigrant Women and Immigration Remedies: Are the Standards Too High?" *Human Rights: Journal of the Section of Individuals Rights and Responsibilities*, vol. 28, Winter 2001, p. 21. Copyright © 2001 by the American Bar Association. Reproduced by permission.

seriousness of the problem or to protect the victim. In many countries, the voices of the victims go unheard, drowned out by age-old traditions that perpetuate the idea that women should serve their husbands no matter how they are treated. Often, the victims' own families do nothing to help the victim of spousal abuse and force her to "endure"—as generations of women have done.

Outside the family network, women also find little assistance in the legal system. Many countries do not codify domestic violence as a separate crime, and some countries regard domestic violence as strictly a family issue to be dealt with in a private manner. In many countries, the law fails to recognize rape by a spouse, a policy that was prevalent in many U.S. states not so long ago. Few countries recognize domestic violence as a crime or have enacted protections for domestic violence victims. And measures that have been enacted all too often fall short due to little or no enforcement. Calling the police in many countries does not ensure any real protection for the victim.

Battered immigrant women in the United States face similar traumas due to both the culture and traditions in which they have been raised. The victim often does not know protection is available, or how to seek it. Many immigrant victims do not speak English and are uninformed about U.S. criminal and immigration laws and systems. Some victims lead very isolated lives in the United States; if they are undocumented, they live secret lives in which they literally have no legal identity and few if any ties to social services, friends, or family. Abusers often compound their abuse by threatening to call the Immigration and Naturalization Service (INS) and have the victim deported if she dares complain about the abuse. The impact of such threat is not exaggerated; undocumented victims know that they are constantly at risk of deportation and fear leaving their children in the United States with the abusing spouse and facing a hostile society upon return to their home country. For example, in many Latin American countries, a woman who returns to her village without her husband and children is ostracized, making it difficult to survive.

The Battered Asylee

As stated above, immigration relief available to battered immigrant women depends on where the abuse occurred. A woman fleeing her country due to domestic violence can, when she enters the United States, seek the remedy of political asylum based on the domestic violence. This makes her subject to asylum laws which derive from U.S. treaty obligations under the United Nations Protocol Relating to the Status of Refugees. To qualify for asylum, an individual must establish that he or she is a "refugee," defined in the Immigration and Naturalization Act (INA) as any person who is unable or unwilling to return to his or her home country due to persecution or a well-founded fear of persecution for one of five reasons: race, religion, nationality, membership in a particular social group, or political opinion.

Asylum claims related to women are often referred to as "gender-based" asylum claims and include any type of persecution that is inflicted on women solely due to their gender. Gender-based asylum claims include rape, female genital mutilation, forced abortion, and domestic violence. Generally, gender-based asylum claims rely on the theories of membership in a social group or political opinion that are found in the definition of a "refugee."

U.S. law recognizes persecution due to gender-related abuse as a basis of asylum. International standards include the United Nations Declaration, the United Nations High Commissioner of Refugee Standards, and the Convention on the Elimination of All Forms of Discrimination Against Women, as well as gender-related persecution guidelines adopted in Canada in 1993. The INS issued its own guidelines, Considerations for Asylum Officers Adjudicating Asylum Claims from Women, in May 1995. They specifically address types of persecution suffered by women and discuss legal arguments tying gender-related persecution to membership in a social group and/or political opinion.

One Woman's Fight for Asylum

The issue of asylum based on domestic violence took on new significance in the 1999 Board of Immigration Appeals (BIA) decision in *In re Matter of R-A* (Interim Decision 3403, BIA 1999). A Guatemalan woman was subjected to extreme domestic violence at the hands of her husband, who beat and raped her repeatedly. He dislocated her jaw, kicked her in the stomach when she was pregnant, whipped her with an electrical cord, and wielded a machete while threatening to cut off her limbs and leave her to spend the rest of her life in a wheelchair. The victim in this case argued that she qualified for asylum because she was persecuted, as evidenced by the domestic violence, based on both a social group and political or imputed political opinion theory.

Although the Immigration Court (an administrative court) granted the victim asylum in the first court proceeding, the BIA reversed the decision, denying the victim's claim on both theories. Especially troubling is that not only did the BIA appear to disregard the INS guidelines and previous gender-based asylum case law, but it also added additional requirements to the asylum standard.

The BIA found that the victim was not a member of a particular persecuted social group, defined as "Guatemalan women who have been involved intimately with Guatemalan male companions, who believe that women are to live under male domination." In rejecting the victim's social group argument, the BIA required that the victim not only prove that she was hurt due to her membership in a group but also that her social group was "cognizable" or easily recognized in society and that there existed a "nexus" between the victim's abuse and the social group. In other words, the BIA required the victim to prove that her spouse specifically abused her due to her membership in a recognized persecuted group.

Under the imputed political opinion theory, the BIA was equally restrictive and denied the victim's asylum claim, stating that she failed to prove that her husband hurt her due to her specific political beliefs.

After efforts made by immigration and women's rights advocates, U.S. Attorney General Janet Reno, on December 7, 2000, issued proposed rules to amend the INS regulations dealing with political asylum and social groups. The drafters recognized that gender could be a basis for a particular social group in an asylum determination and that due to the decision in *R-A*, the issue of women and asylum requires further examination. The regulations allowed for a commentary period through January 2001. Subsequently, Reno ordered the BIA's decision in *R-A* to be vacated and remanded the case back to the BIA for reconsideration with instructions to rehear the case after the proposed regulations become final. It is unclear what form the final law regarding gender-based asylum will take and how this will ultimately affect the decision in *R-A*.

Battered Immigrant Women Living in the United States

The treatment of domestic violence in the asylum context is starkly different from the treatment of domestic violence suffered by immigrant women in the United States. A comparison reveals a double standard in which battered immigrant women living in the United States face a much easier standard than their counterparts fleeing abuse in their home countries.

In 1994, Congress recognized that battered immigrant women who were undocumented, living in the United States, and married to U.S. citizens or legal permanent residents warranted special protection. Traditionally, these women relied on their husbands to petition for their legal status, and had to remain in their good graces. This situation gave the petitioner even more control over his spouse, because her entire immigrant status and ultimate identity in American society depended on his cooperation in signing an affidavit of financial support and attending an interview with his spouse—sometimes years after the application had been filed. The process encouraged undocumented women to stay with their abusers.

Legislation enacted by Congress in 1994 recognized the vulnerability of these battered women. As part of the Violence Against Women's Act (VAWA), Congress amended the INA, allowing battered women who meet certain requirements to seek legal immigration status through a self-petitioning process that does not require the assistance of their abusive spouses. Under this legislation, women must prove the following requirements: (1) legal marriage to a U.S. citizen or legal permanent resident; (2) residence in the United States with the abuser; (3) abuse or extreme cruelty occurring within the U.S.; (4) good moral character of the victim; and (5) extreme hardship if deported. Under this law, women or their attorneys compile the above proof and submit it to the INS. If their self-petitions are approved, the women can immediately apply for work authorization and can eventually apply for legal permanent residency.

In the fall of 2000, the U.S. Congress amended VAWA significantly. The changes allow even more women to qualify for benefits under the law.

A Double Standard

These differing approaches reflect an indefensible double standard. The asylee who flees her country may be held to extraordinarily stringent evidentiary and legal standards. In contrast, the undocumented victim in the United States who meets the requirements is assured protection and legal status by virtue of the fact that the abuse occurred in the United States and that the victim was married to a U.S. citizen or legal permanent resident. If legislators are serious about domestic violence, which the amended VAWA legislation indicates is so, they should work to protect victims of domestic violence regardless of where the abuse occurs. The recent events regarding the proposed gender-based asylum regulations as well as Janet Reno's vacating of the decision in *R-A* may provide parity to these two groups of victims. A double standard serves no one's interests.

ARRESTING BATTERERS DETERS DOMESTIC VIOLENCE

Christopher D. Maxwell, Joel H. Garner, and Jeffrey A. Fagan

Many jurisdictions have instituted laws that require police officers to arrest any person accused of perpetrating domestic violence regardless of the circumstances. In the following selection, Christopher D. Maxwell, Joel H. Garner, and Jeffrey A. Fagan examine research suggesting that arrest is a deterrent to future domestic violence. Batterers who are arrested are much less likely to repeat the crime than those who receive other, less severe responses. Maxwell is an assistant professor at Michigan State University. Garner is a researcher for the Joint Center for Justice Studies. Fagan is the director of the Center for Violence Research and Prevention at Columbia University.

After nearly 20 years of research designed to test the effects of arrest on intimate partner violence, questions persist on whether arrest is more effective at reducing subsequent intimate partner violence than such informal, therapeutic methods as on-scene counseling or temporary separation. The most important research efforts addressing this question were six experiments known collectively as the National Institute of Justice's (NIJ's) Spouse Assault Replication Program (SARP). These field experiments, carried out between 1981 and 1991 by six police departments and research teams, were designed to test empirically whether arrests deterred subsequent violence better than less formal alternatives. . . .

The development of a coherent evaluation of the effectiveness of arrest based on the five experiments with published results was complicated by the differences across the experimental sites in case selection, incident eligibility rules, statistical analysis, and outcome measurements. With these differences, prior attempts to synthesize and understand the substantive diversities among and within the experiments proved difficult. Thus, the full potential of SARP to answer questions about the specific deterrent effect of arrest and the safety of victims has not been realized.

We have previously reviewed and compared the published data

Christopher D. Maxwell, Joel H. Garner, and Jeffrey A. Fagan, "The Effects of the Arrest on Intimate Partner Violence: New Evidence from the Spouse Assault Replication Program," *National Institute of Justice Research Brief*, July 2001.

from the five replication sites that had reported final results to NIJ by 1993. . . . We pointed out that the comparisons were based on infor- mation drawn from different out-come measures, analytical models, and case selection criteria. Furthermore, we asserted that the inconsis- tency between sources and measures across sites was not necessarily because of limitations in the experimental designs, but because the SARP design called for multiple data sources and measures that could capture variations in the nature of the deterrent effect. We argued that conclusions about the deterrent effect of arrest therefore should wait until a more careful statistical analysis was completed, one based on data pooled from all five sites and using standardized measures of intervention and outcome. This Research in Brief summarizes the findings of such a statistical analysis.

We studied the deterrent effect of arrest, using an approach that addressed many problems faced by prior efforts to synthesize the results from SARP. Supported by NIJ and the Centers for Disease Con- trol and Prevention (CDC), the project pooled incidents from the five replication experiments, computed comparable independent and out- come measures from common data intentionally embedded in each experiment, and standardized the experimental designs and statistical models. Using the increased power of the pooled data, this study pro- vides a more consistent, more precise, and less ambiguous estimation of the impact of arrest on intimate partner violence. Key results of this study include the following:

Arrest Works

• Arresting batterers was consistently related to reduced subsequent aggression against female intimate partners, although not all compar- isons met the standard level of statistical significance.

   • Regardless of the statistical significance, the overall size of the relationship between arrest and repeat offending (i.e., the deterrent effect of arrest) was modest when compared to the size of the relation- ship between recidivism and such measures as the batterers' prior criminal record or age.

   • The size of the reduction in subsequent intimate partner aggres- sion did not vary significantly across the five sites. In other words, the benefit of arrest was about equal in regards to reducing aggression in all five sites.

   • Regardless of the type of intervention, most suspects had no sub- sequent criminal offense against their original victim within the fol- lowup period, and most interviewed victims did not report any subse- quent victimization by their batterer.

   • This research found no association between arresting the offender and an increased risk of subsequent aggression against women. . . .

[We conducted a] statistical analysis of the relationship between arrest and several dimensions of intimate partner aggression. The first analysis (prevalence) uses victim interview data to test for the association between arrest and any subsequent aggression during the period between the experimental incident and the last time the victim was interviewed. This model estimated that if their batterers were arrested, about 25 percent fewer female victims than expected reported one or more incidents of aggression. In other words, when the likelihood of failure (reoffending) is estimated for the typical case, about 36 percent of suspects in the arrest group reoffended, compared with 48 percent of suspects in the nonarrest group. This difference was statistically significant while controlling for differences among sites, the length of time the researchers tracked the victims, and characteristics of the suspect and incident. When examining the rates or frequency of aggression, we again found a statistically significant reduction in subsequent aggression that is related to arrest. On average, female victims whose batterers were arrested reported about 30 percent fewer incidences of subsequent aggression than expected over the followup period. Thus, we found a sizable reduction in subsequent aggression reported by victims whose batterers were assigned to the arrest group. However, because these results are based on a subsample of interviewed victims, rather than on the entire sample of eligible cases, the results from the victim interviews alone should be used with some caution because victims not interviewed may have been involved with suspects who responded differently to their intervention.

Location and Suspect Characteristics

Besides the consistent deterrent relationship between arrest and aggression, other factors were consistently related to aggression, but some factors were not. First, compared with the Omaha victims, a significantly smaller percentage of victims from the other sites (except Milwaukee) reported one or more victimizations by the suspect. On average, victims from these three sites also reported less frequent victimization. These differences in the base rates of aggression across the sites, however, did not translate into significantly different relationships between arrest and aggression in the different sites. In other words, the reduction we find in aggression reported by victims whose batterers were assigned an arrest is of about equal size in each site.

In addition to the comparisons we made across the sites, we looked for differences in aggression reported by the victims across several suspect characteristics. These comparisons found that the suspect's age and race were consistently and significantly related to the frequency of subsequent aggression as reported by the victims. These victims reported significantly less aggression when the suspect was older and nonwhite. The suspects' prior arrest records and their marital status with the victim were also consistently related to aggression, but only the prior record was significant in all but one of the analyses. Finally, several other suspect characteristics, such as employment and the use of intoxicants, were inconsistent in the direction of their relationship across the two dimensions of aggression (prevalence and frequency). For example, about 2 percent more victims of employed suspects reported one or more incidents of aggression, though these same victims simultaneously reported about 21 percent fewer incidents of aggression over the followup period.

Examining Police Data

We next examined data collected by police departments to measure aggression by the suspect against the victim. The approach to testing whether arrest was related to officially recorded aggression follows the approach to the victim interviews, except we added a statistical analysis that examined the timing of the first new aggressive incident. Overall, the results based on the police data regarding the effectiveness of arrest are consistent in direction with those based on the victim interview data: A consistent deterrent relationship exists between arrest of the suspect and later aggression while controlling for the differences across the sites, the victim interview process, and suspect characteristics. However, the police data show a far smaller reduction in aggression because of the arrest treatment than what was detected using victim interview data, and none of these relationships reached the traditional level of statistical significance. Specifically, in the first analysis (prevalence), we found about 4 percent fewer than the expected percentage of male suspects in the arrest group with one or more incidents of subsequent aggression during the first 6 months of followup. The second analysis, which tested for the relationship between the intervention and the annual rate of aggression, found a reduction of about 8 percent from the expected number of incidents per year for suspects assigned to the arrest group. Finally, the last analysis, which examined the relationship between arrest and the timing of the first new incident, found that the expected risk of a new incident on any given day after arrest or nonarrest is reduced nearly 10 percent among the arrested suspects. Thus, depending on the dimension of the outcome, the average amount of reported aggression by the suspects dropped by between 4 and 10 percent if they were assigned to the arrest group. . . .

Arrest Has No Negative Long-Term Effect

The average survival [nonoffending] rate throughout the followup period varied substantially by site. On the high end was Omaha, where nearly 90 percent of the suspects had not reoffended by the end of their observation period. On the low side was Dade County, where that figure (the cumulative survival rate) was slightly less than 60 percent. These differences between sites, however, did not result in differences in survival rates by intervention group when the five sites were pooled together. . . . Throughout the followup period, which for some suspects lasted nearly 3 years, batterers who were assigned an arrest had a consistently greater rate of survival (nonoffending) than did those assigned an informal intervention.

This consistent, but small, difference in the survival rate by intervention is important because earlier analysis using data from Milwaukee suggested that arrest may have a significant long-term criminogenic effect. . . . During no particular observation period were the suspects assigned to an arrest more likely to batter their intimate partner than those in the control (nonarrest) group. Thus, among this larger sample of male intimate partner abusers, the survival rate for aggression among those assigned an arrest was never less than that of the control group. . . .

The Effects of Marital Status

Our statistical analysis also showed that the suspects' age, race, employment status, and use of intoxicants at the time of the experimental incident were consistently and significantly related to subsequent aggression against the victim. Contrary to what we found with the victim interviews, white and employed suspects had lower levels of repeat offending according to the police records. Furthermore, suspects who were intoxicated at the time of the experimental incident and those with prior arrests for any crime had, on average, a greater likelihood of aggression recorded by the police. Only the measure of the suspect's marital status with the victim was not consistently or significantly related to aggression. Similar to what we found with the victim interview data, marriage did not appear to provide notable protection against subsequent levels of aggression. Finally, we found that the longer the researchers were able to track the victims for followup interviews, the more initial failures were reported to the police.

In addition to our findings about the relationship between arrest and aggression, we observed some patterns in the pooled data. First, we found a general pattern of cessation or termination of aggression that was only moderately related to the suspects' assigned intervention. According to officially recorded data, less than 30 percent of the suspects, arrested or not, aggressed against the same victim during the followup period. Furthermore, only about 40 percent of the interviewed victims reported subsequent victimization of any measured type by the suspects. Other studies that specifically estimated the rate of desistance from intimate violence have also found similar rates over a 1- to 2-year period.

A second pattern concerns the high concentration of repeat aggression among a small number of batterers. During the 6-month followup, the 3,147 interviewed victims reported more than 9,000 incidents of aggression by the suspects since the initial incident. While most victims reported no new incidents of aggression, about 8 percent of them reported a total number of incidents that represented more than 82 percent of the 9,000 incidents. The same 8 percent also accounted for 28 percent of the 1,387 incidents recorded by the police that involved an interviewed victim. . . .

Reducing Subsequent Aggression

Our multisite pooled analysis of the five replication experiments found good evidence of a consistent and direct, though modest, deterrent effect of arrest on aggression by males against their female intimate partners. The victim interviews indicate that the arrest of the suspect and any subsequent confinement, when compared with the alternative interventions collectively, significantly reduced the expected frequency of subsequent aggression by 30 percent. Similarly, arrest may have reduced by a smaller amount the number of times the police responded to subsequent domestic violence incidents involving the same victim and suspect and may have extended the time between the initial incident and the first subsequent incident. . . .

The findings of this research have several implications for policy. First, our findings provide systematic evidence supporting the argument that arresting male batterers may, independent of other criminal justice sanctions and individual processes, reduce subsequent intimate partner violence. The size and statistical significance of the effect of arrest varied depending on whether the subsequent aggression was measured by victim interviews or police records; even so, in all measures (prevalence, frequency, rate, and time-to-failure), arrest was associated with fewer incidents of subsequent intimate partner aggression. This finding exists during the first several days after the experimental incident regardless of the period of detention, as well as beyond 1 year. The arrested suspects were detained an average of 9 days, but the reduction in aggression associated with arrest did not vary by the length of the suspects' detention. Thus, our research finds no empirical support for the argument that arrest may eventually increase the risk for violence against women. . . .

While arrest reduced the proportion of suspects who reoffended and the frequency with which they reoffended, arrest did not prevent all batterers from continuing their violence against their intimate partners. In fact, we found a small number of victims who have chronically aggressive intimate partners. Future research needs to build on preliminary efforts to accurately predict high-rate repeat offenders and to find methods of helping their victims before they are victimized further.

New Technology Aids the Prosecution of Domestic Violence Cases

Karin Halperin

Digital photography is revolutionizing the prosecution of domestic violence cases, Karin Halperin reports in the following article. As Halperin explains, police departments have traditionally used Polaroid cameras to document the injuries of battered women, but many are now switching to digital cameras, which offer a number of important advantages. Compared to Polaroids, she writes, digital cameras capture clearer and sharper images of bruises, cuts, and other injuries. Furthermore, digital photos can be electronically transmitted from the police precinct to the prosecutor's office within minutes of an arrest, instead of days or weeks later. Since the sharper pictures provide better evidence of the physical trauma, the author relates, prosecutors are often able to file felony-level charges rather than misdemeanor charges against a batterer. Halperin also notes that these digital images are particularly important when victims are reluctant to testify against their abusers, in which case the evidence alone must be sufficient to convict the batterer. Halperin is a freelance journalist based in New York.

Settling into his chair at his cluttered desk on a Tuesday morning, Scott Kessler flicks on his computer and calls up images of injuries. A woman's face emerges, her nose outlined in purplish-blue bruises. Swollen cheeks, lacerated lips, abrasions, scratches, bruised limbs and broken capillaries fill the screen as Kessler, head of the domestic violence bureau in New York's Queens County District Attorney's Office, clicks open recent files, 15 from that morning.

He pauses before an image, pointing out a cut that scores a women's eyelid like an engraving. In another, bumps rise like a ridge from a man's forehead. Kessler zooms in on a woman's back, focusing on a red patch surrounded by black and blue. "You can see the outline of the object used—a stick," he says. "You'll never see anything like that on a Polaroid."

At the 112th Precinct in northern Queens, Officer Linda Rivera holds up a 1.2 megapixel Kodak DC-120 with zoom and built-in viewer. "I was a little nervous when I heard the word 'digital camera,'" she says. "But it's so basic. A victim comes in. We photograph her here or at the hospital. You press two buttons. You see the photo instantly." Before the coming of digital, "we got a lot of dark photos. We'd run out of film. It could be spoiled, discolored." Close-ups, critical for depicting wounds, required cumbersome attachments, some of which had to be fastened to the victim. "This is quicker and less invasive."

Capturing Images of Abuse

Digital imaging, used for mug shots and in fingerprint analysis for years, has edged its way into the touchy territory of domestic violence investigations. "Any agency that has used digital photography for general crime-scene photography is using it for domestic violence, with only a rare exception," says George Reis, whose company, Imaging Forensics, trains federal, state, county and city police forces throughout the country. "Think of all the agencies that have traditionally used Polaroids for domestic violence. Digital is certainly a cheaper and better way to do it."

Convenience isn't the only advantage a digital camera has over its predecessors. For example, Polaroid photographs, taken just after an assault, often fail to depict incipient bruising or the red marks that become more conspicuous in the following days.

"In the past, it was difficult for a prosecutor to convey to a court the extent of the injury, particularly where the injuries are quite serious but don't rise to the level of broken bones or teeth knocked out," says Queens District Attorney Richard Brown, whose office has stepped up its attack on domestic violence since receiving a $3 million grant under the Department of Justice's Violence Against Women Act in 1997.

"[Polaroid] pictures suffer from a number of problems," says Herbert Blitzer, executive director of the Institute for Forensic Imaging at Purdue University. "The lenses put in distortion. The images tend to be dark. It's expensive."

Although 35-millimeter cameras transcend the technical limitations of the Polaroids and might even offer better resolution than some digital models, few patrol officers have the photographic skills to handle them successfully. "They often make several mistakes, and the images are no good," says Blitzer.

"They often get too close to the subject, and so I had blurry pictures," says Timothy Johnson, deputy district attorney in the sex crimes and domestic violence unit in the Boulder (Colorado) District Attorney's Office. Six of the nine police agencies in his jurisdiction switched to digital cameras around 2000. "In strangulation cases, which in Boulder County is a growing method of choice, the injuries didn't photograph. They overdo the flash. How do you prove strangulation if you don't have marks?"

Kessler, examining an 8-by-10-inch digital printout of a woman with a cut lip, says, "The color is better, especially for women with different complexions," a fact not lost in Queens, whose 167 nationalities make it the most ethnically diverse county in the country.

Most importantly, the photographs can be downloaded and zapped from the precinct to the prosecutor's office within minutes of an arrest, instead of days or weeks. "We can print them out and present them at arraignments," says Kessler, whose staff handles about 4,500 misdemeanor and 500 felony cases a year. "They're strong evidence in bail applications."

A Useful New Tool

Whether technology can make a dent in domestic violence, a complicated nexus of behaviors that includes battering and injury, psychological intimidation and sexual assault between intimate partners, is anyone's guess. According to the Bureau of Justice Statistics, 1.3 million women and 835,000 men are physically assaulted by an intimate partner every year in the United States. Will incremental advances in technology make a real difference in those figures? And, wonder some critics, is the malleability of digital imaging a potential weakness for getting evidence accepted in court?

Police and prosecutors dismiss the possible drawbacks of the new technology. They believe that high-quality digital photographs received early in the legal labyrinth can make an impact—especially in the complex world of domestic violence, where victims are often unwilling to testify, and pictures have to do the talking.

"There's strong evidence that they're a good tool in fighting domestic violence," says Kessler.

Queens is the first and so far the only area of New York City using digital cameras to photograph domestic violence victims. Working with the district attorney's office, the New York Police Department (NYPD) weaned the county's 16 police precincts off their instant Polaroids in 2001, starting with three digital cameras in three precincts, then adding five more a few months later, then eight more, until every domestic violence unit in every Queens station house had one. "They were doing digital photographs of offenders. We figured if we could get documentary evidence of what an offender looked like . . . we should at least be documenting what the victim looked like at the time of the crime," says Lucia Raiford, director of the NYPD's domestic violence unit, which bought the cameras.

George Reis, who is also a crime scene investigator for the Newport Beach (California) Police Department, estimates that up to a quarter of the 18,500 police departments in the United States have swapped their 35-millimeter and instant Polaroids for digitals. "Digital photography probably started in forensic applications on the West Coast and moved east," he says. His own force went digital in 1991. "You'll see it much more in agencies that are 200 people or less. It's an expensive transition for a large agency—they have to buy so much more of everything—and it's hard to coordinate."

Better Evidence

David Adkins, principal photographer in charge of the Scientific Identification Division at the Los Angeles Police Department (LAPD), says digital cameras encourage officers to take more photographs when out on domestic violence calls. "People are conscious of the cost of Polaroids at $1 or $1.25 apiece, and they'll take three or four and feel that's enough. They're excited about the digital technology. They know they can take as many as they want, because there's this perception that digital photography is free photography." When the perpetrator is confronted with the barrage of evidence, "a lot more plea bargains come out of it."

Digital documentation has also resulted in stiffer charges. Deputy District Attorney Johnson says he has filed more felony-level charges and more high-level third degree assault charges when he provides digital photographs. "They're supported by better evidence," he says, describing a case in which a husband knocked down his wife and strangled her into unconsciousness as her face bled. The police took 27 initial photographs, along with follow-up pictures three days later. "Her left eye was swollen shut, and her neck had inflamed to about twice its size because of the trauma," says Johnson. "Because of the digital technology, I was able to see that faster and filed a felony assault instead of a misdemeanor assault."

Prosecutors hope the digital photographs will help them sidestep one of the touchiest issues in pursuing domestic violence cases—the victim's reluctance or refusal to file a complaint or testify, and the tendency to retract a complaint or testimony later. Sometimes it's for economic reasons if the batterer is the main wage-earner. In localities like Queens with large immigrant populations, victims might have a genuine fear of the Immigration and Naturalization Service (INS). "The victim might not speak English or understand what is going on. They're not sure what's going to happen to them in court," says Rita Asen, director of Queens Criminal and Supreme Court programs for Safe Horizon, which counsels victims of crime and abuse. Often, the victim fears retaliation from the defendant or the defendant's family. "It's a tough decision for them to make," says Wanda Lucibello, chief of the special victims unit in the Kings County–Brooklyn District Attorney's Office. "The punishment is pretty minimal in a misdemeanor. We're asking women to participate in cases where there's not a big hammer hanging over the guy's head."

Prosecuting "Victimless" Cases

In these victimless, or more euphemistically, evidence-intensive prosecutions, the digital photographs become important, especially in "no-drop" jurisdictions, where prosecutors can pursue a case without the victim's consent, complaint or testimony.

"The evidence can sometimes be put together in a way that can stand on its own," says Lucibello. "Our hope is that these cases can go forward without the victim's participation when we think that's going to be the safe, sound way to go. The injuries can be documented, the scene can be documented—the broken furniture, the door that's got the dent marks in it because somebody tried to kick it open, the table that got broken, the chair leg that might have been used to menace the victim, the doors, the tables, the blood that gets left behind. All of that is the way these cases get prosecuted without the victim."

If the photographic evidence is strong enough, the police officer who responded to the emergency call can testify for the victim. The "excited utterance" exception to the hearsay rule allows the police officer to testify about statements the victim made right after the assault if it can be proved she made them while still under duress. "We often have a difficult time because what evidence do we have other than the officer saying, she looked scared, she looked upset," says Johnson. "With the digital photography, we're getting higher-quality pictures during the interview. We're able to get pictures of the victim crying, with tears in the eyes. Getting these 'excited utterances' in is a huge victory for us in these victimless prosecutions."

Few Challenges to Digital Technology

One oft-mentioned criticism of digital photography is its malleability—anything digital can be changed with ease, which raises questions about the admissibility of digital images as evidence. But despite their malleability, digital images have faced few court challenges. Federal and state rules of evidence have stretched to accommodate the technology. In the 1995 precedent-setting case of the *State of Washington vs. Eric Hayden*, the court admitted into evidence digital photographs of fingerprints it knew had been altered (police investigators had enhanced latent hand and fingerprints found on a bedsheet through a variety of techniques the court deemed scientifically valid—NASA scientists had developed the technology in the 1960s to record satellite signals), and convicted Hayden of murder. The state appellate court upheld the decision three years later.

As a result, courts regularly admit digital images, even when they know they've been changed. "Just as with traditional photographic images, digital images generally need to be altered to represent what the person who photographed them saw," says Reis. "Altering an image is not necessarily a bad thing; it's a required thing in many cases."

But every new touch-up tool from Photoshop, Photo-Paint, Photo Studio and the like raises questions, provoking periodic cries to amend the "evidentiary codes."

"Digital photographs are easy to manipulate by using the clone stamp or multiple other tools," says David Spraggs, a detective with the Boulder (Colorado) Police Department, who oversaw his agency's switch to digital.

Not everyone agrees it can be done effortlessly, though. "It's what I call the goat's head syndrome," says the LAPD's Adkins. "It's the Hollywood version and the belief that you can put a goat's head on a donkey and no one can tell the difference. Well, it's not so easy to do that. You can make those changes, but you have to work quite a long time with the right tools to do that."

Spraggs, who teaches digital forensic photography and crime scene investigation, uses Adobe Photoshop daily to sharpen, resize, adjust the color or correct for faulty focus or camera settings. Sometimes he also uses GretagMacbeth's color-gauging tools.

Accurately Representing the Crime Scene

Color is particularly important when preparing photographs of domestic violence or assault victims, he says. "We don't want to make the injury seem worse than it is or less serious than it is. We make the images look like a more accurate representation of what the photographer saw at the scene." Spraggs saves the original images on a writable CD-ROM, makes his changes on working copies and records every step he takes to enhance the original image on Photoshop's Action Palette. He then prints and attaches the record to the photograph and sends it to court. Any investigator can replicate Spragg's changes and reproduce the photograph from the original file, just like in a scientific experiment. Call it ethical enhancement. "The distinction is between changing the quality and changing the content," says Reis. "You never change the content."

But, as Spraggs admits, the line can at times become gray. He offers his favorite reply: Traditional film-based images, which were always retouchable, can now be altered just as easily as digital photographs. "You can scan that film into a computer, turn it into a digital file and manipulate it in Photoshop," he explains, and, with a device called a film recorder, reconvert the altered digitized files to film. "Basically, the technology goes full circle, and has gotten to the point where any image can be questioned." In other words, if film is no longer "safe," why worry about digital?

Always ready to fill a vacuum, vendors have stepped in with image-security software in the form of "tamper-proof" encoded formats that bolt in the picture at the time it's captured, but most forensics experts deem such precautions costly and unnecessary. "It gives a certain amount of comfort, but most of the software can be defeated in one way or another," says Steven B. Staggs, author of Crime Scene and Evidence Photographer's Guide and a forensic photography instructor for 17 years.

Instead, Staggs and Spraggs preach such low-tech steps as developing standard operating procedures, maintaining chains of custody for the images, preserving the original, keeping logs, restricting access— all basic guidelines similar to those developed by the FBI's Scientific Working Group on Imaging Technologies, or SWIGIT.

"If people buy into your protocols, you're fine," says Staggs.

Courtroom acceptance of an image, whether a drawing, a conventional photograph, a videotape or a digital photograph, has hinged on "authentication," which requires only that an on-the-scene witness testify that the photograph is an accurate representation of what he or she saw. "That statement takes the onus off the means by which [the photograph] was produced and puts it on the testimony of the witness, because the witness testifies in fear of perjury," says Blitzer, who sits on the SWIGIT committee. "The technology is a backseat issue. You can't put a picture in jail, but you can put a false witness in jail."

"Victimless" Prosecution Is Controversial

But while the technology itself doesn't appear to be riling defense attorneys, the notion of victimless prosecution—the idea that photographs can substitute for an unwilling plaintiff—does raise serious hackles.

"They've tried to do it, and we scream," says Steven Silverblatt, supervising attorney for the Queens Legal Aid Society. "The defendant feels deprived of his constitutional rights when this happens. They're looking for ways to make the case without the victim. If they want to take better pictures, great. No one can say that better photography is damaging, provided they don't pressure people who don't want to press charges into doing so. People have complicated relationships. They might want to solve their problems on their own. It's not that we approve of domestic violence, but these solutions can produce results a complaining witness doesn't want."

Unlike armed robbery or other attacks by strangers, domestic violence cases "are complicated in a way that a lot of other serious crimes are not," says Holly Maguigan, a professor of clinical law at New York University who studies the criminal prosecution of domestic violence cases. "Sometimes victims don't press charges because prosecution isn't the way out of a bad situation for them. It might not be a particular woman's own best route to safety. Since the police cannot provide 'round-the-clock protection to people, there's a way in which it's hard not to credit her opinion."

Prosecutors say they stay mindful of this. "With some people, the prosecution is only part of the big picture," says Lucibello, whose office will soon be relying on digital photographs. "But you need to be ready to go forward without the victim's participation. I can think of examples where the hair would stand up on the back of your neck if you thought there wasn't going to be a prosecution. But that doesn't mean you'll always take that route—maybe it's working with an advocate and putting together a safety plan. Even if you decide at the end that prosecution is not the safest thing to do, the digital cameras give you the ability. They're something to go into the arsenal of weapons."

CHAPTER 3

SOCIETY'S RESPONSE TO VIOLENCE AGAINST WOMEN

SOCIAL SERVICES FOR VICTIMS AND PERPETRATORS OF DOMESTIC VIOLENCE

Dawn Bradley Berry

Lawyer and author Dawn Bradley Berry describes some of the social services available to battered women in the following excerpt from *The Domestic Violence Sourcebook*. According to Berry, shelters present the best strategy for ensuring the immediate safety of a battered woman and her children by providing short-term emergency housing. In addition, she notes, most shelters offer material assistance (such as food, clothing, and medical care), counseling, legal aid, and referrals to other social service agencies. Equally important are programs designed to treat abusive men. Treatment programs are most effective, the author contends, when they require long-term participation, apply direct and meaningful consequences for the abuse, and force batterers to take responsibility for their behavior. Although social services for battered women and their abusers are chronically under-funded, these programs are capable of saving individual lives and helping to break the cycle of violence, Berry concludes.

Through the grassroots efforts of the battered women's movement, a wide variety of services are now available for everyone damaged by domestic violence—the victims, the abusers, and the children. All states now have domestic violence coalitions that provide assistance, information, and referrals. Yet where a battered woman lives can make a world of difference in how she is treated by police, courts, and other institutions, as well as what services are available and how accessible they are. Fortunately, help for those in abusive relationships is becoming more abundant and more effective. Coordination of efforts between the various helping agencies—police, shelters, courts, and others—has greatly improved overall, so more of the available services are streamlined and communicating with one another. Even small, rural communities are beginning to establish shelters and safe house networks, counseling programs, and other services. Many of the older programs with proven track records have begun producing low-cost training materials and conducting seminars to teach people in other communities how to use the same techniques in their own areas.

Battered Women's Shelters

The most important element of safety, especially for a woman who fears her abuser might try to kill her, is to make herself unavailable to her pursuer. Battered women's shelters are often the best and most available strategy to achieve this goal. Shelters are run by professionals who have the wisdom to understand the need for secrecy, who know that safety is the paramount issue before justice, before the future, before any of the other important, but not life-and-death issues can be addressed.

There are over eighteen hundred shelters for battered women in America today, and countless other safe houses (private homes) or temporary facilities in churches, community centers, and YWCAs across the nation. The shortage of shelters for battered women and their children is still desperate. In 1996, there were only about eighteen hundred shelters nationwide. For every two women accepted, five were turned away. And for every two children sheltered, eight were refused. The locations of shelters are usually kept secret to protect the residents from angry husbands. Telephone numbers are listed in local directories under "Shelter," "Social Services," "Women's Services," "Crisis Intervention," or similar headings. Numbers are also posted in areas such as women's bookstores, libraries, laundromats, bus stops, and other public places.

Shelters are best known for what their name implies—emergency, short-term housing for women in crisis. Shelters usually allow residents to stay for thirty days. The average length of stay is about two weeks.

First and foremost, shelters save lives. Yet most shelters, and the organizations that run them, provide far more than crisis intervention. For example, the Women's Community Association in Albuquerque, New Mexico, provides a shelter for battered women and their children free of charge; a twenty-four-hour crisis hotline; emergency transportation; food, clothing, and medical attention; individual and group counseling; employment and housing referrals; legal advocacy; counseling for children; battered women support groups; and parenting programs. For a low fee, it also offers a twenty-four-week program for abusers, which includes a crisis hotline; group, individual, children's, and partner counseling; and parenting programs. All services of the Women's Community Association are also offered in Spanish.

While the Albuquerque shelter offers more services than many, especially those in smaller communities, nearly all shelters provide some kind of individual and group counseling, as well as referrals to other agencies. These services are generally available to women who are not staying in the shelter, as well as those who are. Other shelters may offer housing assistance, legal assistance, and on-site help with public aid and other social service applications. Most shelters today are part of a larger system of services that work together to help a woman face the complex array of legal, social, and personal needs she encounters when fleeing an abusive marriage. Sometimes court or victim advocates visit shelters to let women know their rights, and to help them pursue prosecution of the abuser and/or obtain a protective order. Research by law enforcement agencies has shown that when more shelters are available for battered women, fewer male partners are killed by women defending themselves.

Some abuse survivors and the professionals who work with them believe the support of other women who have survived abuse is the single most important key to recovering from the damage caused by violence. Women who meet in shelters very often develop a sense of sisterhood with others who have suffered in similar ways. Women who share housework, child care, and a common plight often find a strong bond that leads to ongoing support and friendship lasting well beyond the duration of the shelter stay. Many lifelong friendships have been forged beneath the roofs of emergency housing facilities.

Providing Help for All Battered Women

Today, most larger cities have shelters or safe houses, and many programs centered in cities serve outlying areas as well. In Albuquerque, for example, the Women's Community Association serves a tri-county area. Through two outreach sites, the program has expanded its services to accommodate a vast, sparsely populated rural area, including transportation of victims to the shelter at any time of the day or night. "Sometimes we have to drive 150 miles to go get someone at three o'clock in the morning, but if that's what it takes, we'll do it," says Catherine Chaney, director of the programs. Women's shelters are also beginning to address the common problem of substance abuse among battered women, rather than enforce blanket rules that those who use alcohol or drugs will be evicted. Women may react differently to traditional treatment methods, most developed for men, and need a different kind of treatment. Their practical problems must also be considered. For example, a woman who can't get child care and misses a meeting as a result might be told she is in denial, when she is not. Female alcoholics suffer more stigma than males, and abused women often face a double stigma—they are asked why are they using, and why don't they leave. The right question would be how can we help her stop and leave. A victim who conquers her substance problem is more likely to stay out of an abusive situation.

The University of New Mexico has begun research to determine what works for women with both domestic violence and substance abuse problems. Working with the Women's Community Association, the study seeks to identify the resiliency that keeps the survivors out, and what aid from the community, peers, and treatment programs best helps them stay both sober and free. As part of the study, one shelter plans to implement a program that will offer resident special substance-abuse counseling.

Support is also essential for women who have left a shelter for alternative housing, those trying to make this transition, and those who have never been in a shelter. Many shelters and social service agencies provide such support as counseling and group therapy, information and assistance on such issues as housing, and referrals to all who need it.

Diverse needs should also be recognized in addressing the question of how to help battered women. As the Battered/Formerly Battered Women's Task Force [of the National Coalition Against Domestic Violence (NCADV)] emphasizes, there are many ways abuse survivors work to empower and heal themselves, and while traditional mental health approaches do work best for some, the importance of alternative methods such as art, spirituality, political involvement, study, and physical achievements should not be discounted.

The services provided by shelters is invaluable. Women who stay in a shelter or safe house are more likely to leave their abusers. Even the most basic shelters serve not only as a refuge, but as a community where women find support, encouragement, and an end to isolation and helplessness. Shelters often serve as a point of entry into the system of services for women who are leaving abusive marriages, whether or not they stay at the shelter. Police in many cities provide transportation to shelters for women fleeing the scene of a domestic assault.

Most shelters receive some funding from the state, local, or federal government. Some states use part of the fees charged for marriage licenses to fund shelters. Others contribute from fines charged as part of abuser sentences, or charge fees to abusers in related counseling programs. All, however, must rely on private sources as well.

More Services Are Still Needed

Shelters are chronically underfunded, understaffed, and incapable of serving all the women and children who need them. In some cities, as many as six out of seven must be turned away. Most shelters must rely, at least in part, on volunteer help and donations. Many former shelter residents go on to volunteer or work in a paid capacity for the shelter and find such work a rewarding part of building a new life.

In many areas, better assistance to victims is needed after the initial escape, for example, after her time limit at the shelter runs out. This is when many women return to their abuser because they feel they have no place else to go. Ironically, many victims feel safer if they return to a dangerous home than if they must continually be on the lookout for a stalker.

New York City councilwoman Ronnie Eldridge has proposed a unique idea—rather than sending women and children to shelters, why not remove the abuser from the home? Eldridge has suggested that batterers be arrested and then either incarcerated or paroled into a batterer's treatment program in which he is placed in a dormitory-type facility while he participates in a mandatory treatment program. The victims and their children should not be forced to undergo the additional trauma of leaving their familiar home, possessions and surroundings. Such a system would be more cost-effective because fewer beds would be required (the majority of abused women flee with one or more children) and more fair, since it would be the criminal, not the victim, who is penalized. . . .

Batterers' Programs

Over the past twenty years, many community mental health agencies have developed treatment and education programs for abusive men, often with the help of other such groups that have been through a trial and error period and learned what types of help are most likely to be effective. Many of these programs started in conjunction with new approaches to domestic violence in the criminal justice system. Today, men who plead or are found guilty of battering are often required to choose between treatment or jail.

The approaches of these programs, and their success rates, vary. Generally, the longer programs, which require abusers to attend therapy sessions for at least six months, have better results over the long term than those that require only a few sessions. Some combine group and individual counseling; some break the program down into separate components such as education, dynamics of the violent relationship, and anger management. Many require screening for substance abuse and separate treatment for alcoholism or drug abuse if necessary.

There do seem to be three points that virtually all experts agree are necessary for successful treatment of abusers. First, the man must admit his responsibility for the abuse. He must realize that it was wrong, accept that he cannot control other adults with equal rights, and want to change his behavior. Second, there must be some demonstrated consequences for the abuse. Many programs require all abusers to spend at least one night in jail, some longer, depending on the circumstances of the case. Even one night behind bars can make a strong impression. Third, there must be accountability that continues beyond the mandatory treatment period—through continued group support, court monitoring of a longer term of probation, or a court order strictly prohibiting harassment or violence and providing strict penalties for violation.

Any abuser's program will be most effective if it starts promptly after arrest and lasts several months or longer. The Duluth, Minnesota program, recognized as one of the best, lasts twenty-six weeks. Sixty percent of the men who go through the program have not been charged with assault again, according to a follow-up study. Men who enter programs under court order, with sanctions for unexcused absences and automatic jail time for quitting continued abuse, seem to achieve better results. Also, the earlier this intervention happens, the greater the chance of success: a man who gets into counseling after the first or second assault is more likely to reform than one who has been battering and getting away with it for twenty years.

Techniques to Control Anger

Maryland psychologist Steven Stosny, Ph.D., developed an effective program based on the theory that most batterers cannot sustain attachments, so as a result they become overwhelmed with feelings of guilt, shame, and abandonment, which they seek to regulate through aggression. His five-step technique, called HEALS, is the basis for a remarkably effective treatment program that he describes as teaching Mr. Hyde to remember what Dr. Jekyll learned. The twelve-week program boasts impressive follow-up statistics, with 86 percent of the participants having ended the physical abuse a year after treatment, and 73 percent free of emotional and verbal abuse.

Stosny's technique starts with the concept of "Heal," in which men are taught that blame is powerless, while compassion is the true power, with the ability to heal. The men are next taught to "Explain" to themselves the core hurt masked by their anger, the pain that motivates abusive behavior—feelings of being unimportant, disregarded, guilty, devalued, rejected, powerless, unlovable. They are taught to "Apply" self-compassion—instead of reacting instinctively to an insult or comment from his wife with anger. Finally, the man is taught to move into feeling "Love" for himself and his partner, and to present his true position without blaming or attacking her—to heal the core hurt through love rather than anger, compassion instead of abuse.

HEALS participants practice these techniques by remembering an incident that made them feel angry, letting themselves experience the anger, then following the HEAL steps, twelve times a day for four weeks. Stosny explains that this method works almost like a vaccination, by creating an immunity to the core hurt that triggers the abusive behavior.

Although Stosny is quite successful in teaching his clients to end their abusive behavior, he is also realistic in his view of the difficulty of mending formerly abusive relationships. He emphasizes the importance of putting the safety of the victim first, and tells the women involved with these men that there is more to life than not being abused. He and his colleagues counsel these women to understand that while it's unlikely they will be abused any more, it's also unlikely that they will have a very good relationship with their abuser. He reports that the separation rate is higher than average for program participants, with 46 percent of the wives leaving their husbands.

Key Elements of Successful Programs

An ongoing study on batterer intervention that works, conducted by the National Centers for Disease Control in Atlanta, has confirmed the long-held view that the earlier intervention occurs, the easier it will be to change a batterer's behavior. The study has also found that substance abuse treatment must be combined with violence treatment where it is required, and that programs that allow the batterer to choose any counselor are not effective—it takes six months to two years of work with a trained counselor. Some programs are beginning to use peer sponsorship, similar to that used by Alcoholics Anonymous, which hasn't been studied extensively, but appears to be helpful for some.

Programs for abusive men have several advantages over incarceration alone. Sentencing of abusers has the greatest effect if it includes both sanctions and treatment. A man who feels guilty and remorseful after the battering will often be responsive to counseling if he can start while still in this part of the cycle. He can keep his job, and if the woman wants to maintain the relationship, the couple can have a better chance of a safe and successful attempt to salvage it.

Companies Address Domestic Violence in the Workplace

Stephanie Armour

In the following article, *USA Today* reporter Stephanie Armour examines the issue of battered women in the workplace. Armour reveals that abusive partners frequently attempt to sabotage their victims' employment by harassing them on the job. However, she states, a company that fires a woman because of her batterer's disruptive behavior risks being sued for violating her rights. Some workplaces have begun to deal directly with domestic violence through innovative outreach programs, the author writes. These companies offer support to employees who are victims of abuse by providing paid leave time, security escorts, and literature on shelters and other resources for battered women. According to Armour, corporate-sponsored employee-assistance programs are in a unique position to assist battered women in finding the help they need.

On a moonlit August night, Marsha Midgette arrived at her Wal-Mart job in Pottstown, Pa.

A would-be killer was waiting for her.

Around 9:30 P.M., a gunman chased her into an employee training room and shot her in the head.

But this wasn't a case of random workplace violence. The shooter was her husband, Bryan, who had bought the bullets just a half-hour earlier from the same store where his estranged wife worked, according to a lawsuit she filed.

Marsha survived with brain damage. She is suing Wal-Mart because she says not enough was done to protect her. Wal-Mart did not return calls seeking comment.

Her husband killed himself at the scene.

The case highlights a growing issue for employers: As more women join the labor force, domestic violence is moving from the home into the workplace. And it's taking a toll. Roughly 20,000 employees are threatened or attacked in the workplace every year by spouses or partners, according to a review of 1992–96 statistics by the Justice Department.

More than 70% of domestic violence victims are also harassed while at work by spouses or significant others, according to the American Institute on Domestic Violence. Studies show domestic violence—physical violence by a current or former spouse, boyfriend or girlfriend—costs employers $3 billion to $5 billion annually in higher turnover, lower productivity, absenteeism and health and safety expenses.

A Taboo Subject

Despite such consequences, domestic violence is a topic that remains taboo. While roughly 65% of senior executives say they feel those problems could be alleviated if their companies tackled domestic abuse, a 2002 report by the Partnership for Prevention found most firms do nothing at all. A small number of employers are addressing the problem with innovative outreach efforts, educational programs and new policies—a trend that victim advocates hope will spur other companies to get involved.

"It's still such a stigmatized issue," says Maris Bondi, a senior health analyst and primary author of the study by the Washington-based membership association. "No one wants to talk about it, admit it. That's too bad, because employers who get involved can make a difference."

For victims, the inattention compounds problems. Some insurance companies have sought to deny medical coverage related to domestic abuse by classifying it as a pre-existing condition. Victims who need to leave work for court appearances have been denied the time off. Others have been fired after spouses, boyfriends or girlfriends showed up at work or made harassing calls.

That's what happened to Kathy Evsich. Because she needed to stash money so she could flee her abuser, Evsich took a job as a waitress in a family-owned restaurant. She says she couldn't get a restraining order because she was living with her husband and couldn't afford to leave.

In 1999, her husband began parking outside and watching her through the windows, according to testimony Evsich gave in July 2002 at a hearing before a U.S. Senate committee. He would come into the restaurant and demand that she leave. He also called and threatened the owner.

Evsich says she paid the price for his behavior: She was fired.

"(My employer) looked at me and said, 'Goodbye,'" says Evsich, 35, a mother of two in Swannanoa, N.C. "I needed that job."

Evsich got another job at a credit union. But her spouse came back: On her first day, he began driving back and forth in front of her workplace and blaring his car horn. He called every five minutes and parked outside the window. On her third day on the job, Evsich testified, she was fired again. She says her employer told her they couldn't tolerate what her husband was doing.

On Nov. 10, 1999, Evsich was attacked by him and, according to her testimony, seriously wounded. She is now disabled. She and her husband are divorced.

"Employers don't want to deal with it. It's not their problem," Evsich says. "It's so important they do something. Domestic violence is a hidden crime. It's scary. It affects all status levels—doctors, lawyers and poor people, too."

Zero Tolerance for Abusers

Those companies that are getting involved take a variety of steps. Some are drafting zero-tolerance policies that include domestic violence. The policies offer protection and security to victims and warn abusers who work at the firm that they can be fired for using company e-mail or phones to threaten or harass.

Other companies are encouraging workers to volunteer at domestic shelters, giving panic buttons to receptionists and training managers to spot victims among their employees. When the ex-boyfriend of a summer intern at Liz Claiborne began stalking her, the apparel company's security personnel escorted her to the train and waited for her to call to tell them she was home safe.

Consumer electronics company Harman International Industries began its domestic violence prevention program after the death of Teresa Duran. The 56-year-old had been with the Northridge, Calif., division of the company for 24 years. Her husband was convicted of murdering her in May 2001 as she left work. He followed her home and stabbed her more than 20 times before running over her with his minivan.

"That sparked our program," says Lynn Harman, corporate counsel. "We had to do something."

The company wrote up a domestic violence policy that will be in all the company handbooks. Most of the roughly 3,500 U.S. employees went through training on domestic violence issues. And if an employee comes forward to say he or she is being threatened by violence, the company will work with that employee to be sure his or her performance review isn't adversely affected because of related lateness or productivity issues.

While still in its infancy, the program has had an impact.

"People were finally coming forward because they know the company wouldn't fire them," Harman says. The company makes audio products that carry the names Harman/Kardon, JBL, Infinity and others. "They had some pretty horrific stories. It was staggering."

Raising Awareness

But it's not always easy. Companies that try to address the issue have found employees reluctant to attend talks on domestic violence. Instead, companies such as Verizon Wireless have held learning programs on general subjects, such as violence and teen dating, where domestic violence is a component of the discussion but not the main topic.

Instead of making pamphlets on domestic violence available only in the human resources department, the company has left literature in bathrooms where women might feel more comfortable picking it up.

"It's hard to get a lot of people to come to a session on domestic violence," says spokeswoman Andrea Linskey. "But if we create an environment where people feel comfortable talking about it, it may encourage a victim to come forward."

It's an approach some other companies are taking. For example:

• At Dallas-based skin-care and cosmetics company Mary Kay, employees are encouraged to volunteer in domestic violence programs. The goal: to raise awareness and encourage victims who work for the company to come forward. Employees have donated books to domestic violence shelters and assembled care packages for families fleeing abusers.

• Illinois State University in Normal has sent inserts in credit union mail with information on relationships and domestic violence and used liaisons in each department to help address the issue.

The organization has been touched by domestic violence: An employee on campus was shot and killed by her husband.

"The only reason it's hard to sell is (that) it's awkward and uncomfortable. It's a difficult issue to bring up," says Marabeth Clapp, assistant vice president of business services and human resources.

• After an employee was killed in 1996 by her ex-husband, McKee Foods in Gentry, Ark., began its domestic violence prevention efforts—dubbed Project Ruth in her memory. Supervisors are instructed annually about how to detect signs a staffer is being abused. The maker of Little Debbie snack foods has juggled work schedules, allowed women who were threatened to park in special spots near the building and helped employees get to shelters.

Carmen Burasco, who serves as employee health services and wellness administrator, speaks with women believed to be at risk.

"A lot of times, they'll talk to me but not a supervisor," Burasco says. "Recently, someone came and said, 'I'm in a situation,' and we called the police to talk with her."

Such programs pay off. American Express, which has a domestic violence prevention program, had an employee who was being harassed. They gave her a cellphone, which she used to call 911 while being followed on the highway. The dispatcher directed her to a police station, and the man was arrested.

Businesses Have Legal Responsibilities

Legal experts say employers who do nothing after an employee complains about potential threats could be found liable for failing to keep workers safe. Indiana has passed a law that allows companies to get restraining orders against anyone who is threatening an employee.

Victims have some protection. Women with psychological or physical injuries might legally be able to take time off under the Family and Medical Leave Act or short-term disability.

And legal experts say firing a woman because of a husband's or boyfriend's threatening behavior might amount to sex discrimination, giving victims grounds to sue.

"It's an area that hasn't been explored much in the law," says Jennifer Brown, vice president and legal director of the NOW [National Organization for Women] Legal Defense and Education Fund in New York.

Proposed federal legislation would allow victims to take temporary unpaid leave, get unemployment if they lost their jobs because of violence and prohibit companies from discriminating against victims.

But without that protection, some victims say employers are falling short.

Melissa Rimel, 31, says her abuser made it hard for her to focus on work. She felt embarrassed, she says, in front of co-workers. Her ex-husband abused and threatened her for more than eight years, according to her petition for a restraining order granted in 1999.

She says the effects of the abuse caused her to be fired from a job at a grocery.

"You just want to cower down," says Rimel, mother of three children in Pueblo, Colo. "I was embarrassed more than anything. If employees are missing work, I can understand it's a problem, but companies should find some way to help."

THE IMPORTANCE OF TAILORING SOCIAL SERVICES TO SPECIFIC POPULATIONS

Dylan Foley

Although much progress has been made in providing social services for battered women, Dylan Foley observes in the following article that women from certain populations have a difficult time obtaining the assistance they need. In particular, he looks at two underserved groups of victims—lesbians and immigrant Arab women. Lesbians face difficulties in having their legal rights recognized, Foley states, and they often experience discrimination from service workers unused to dealing with same-sex domestic violence cases. Immigrant Arab women, on the other hand, encounter problems arising from intense cultural isolation, language barriers, and racial or religious discrimination, the author reports. Foley also profiles the Safe Homes Project in Brooklyn, New York, which tailors its intervention programs to the specific needs of these women. A one-size-fits-all approach no longer works for victims of domestic violence, he concludes. Foley is a freelance writer in New York and a frequent contributor to *City Limits*.

One night, while Barbara was asleep in her New York City apartment, her girlfriend attacked her, stabbing her in the forehead. She survived the attack with 50 stitches, but that was just the beginning of her ordeal. For Barbara, a lesbian, the battered women's shelter she fled to wasn't much of a respite.

She was sent to an out-of-state women's shelter where the staff instructed her not to tell the other residents that her attacker was a woman. They also made derogatory comments about lesbians, breaking their promise of confidentiality and telling other shelter residents she was gay. Then they failed to protect her when she was insulted and humiliated by the other women.

Luckily, Barbara was transferred back to Brooklyn to a shelter that specializes in helping battered lesbians. There she got counseling, sympathy and help in finding safe permanent housing.

The women's shelter that Barbara went to is run by the Park Slope Safe Homes Project, a 22-year-old battered women's program that started with a small group of women offering spare bedrooms to other women running from their abusive husbands. It has since evolved into a $700,000-a-year non-profit with 13 staff members, a hotline and two small shelters.

And as the demographics of the women in southern Brooklyn have changed, the organization adapted to fit. "In the beginning Safe Homes primarily served middle-class white women," says executive director Cynthia Dansby. "Now we get women from all over the city. We are seeing younger women who've had their children young. We've had women who've been on the streets."

The lesbian project that helped Barbara started up in the early 1990s, and Safe Homes has since begun a specialty program for another new Brooklyn community: immigrant Arab women. The two populations are very different, but both run into trouble in the battered women's social services system. For lesbians, domestic violence is still a taboo subject. They have problems getting their legal rights recognized, and the police and shelter system are unresponsive, even hostile. For Arab women, there is intense cultural isolation, a lack of Arabic-speaking social service workers and discrimination.

Meeting Special Needs

Recognizing that a one-size-fits-all attitude no longer works for domestic violence prevention and counseling, the Safe Homes Project developed programs that are specially suited to the changing needs of Brooklyn women. And as the women who staff these programs have discovered, it takes a particular mix of compassion and pragmatism to get these women the help they need.

Lesbians often have a difficult time in social services and legal systems that are designed for heterosexual couples, says Safe Homes staffer Judy Yu, a young, politically active lesbian. Cops, judges and social workers are often unsympathetic or even downright rude.

"One of our clients was applying for welfare," remembers Yu. "The social worker said 'You let yourself get beaten up by a woman?' and started laughing."

Yu says that police officers can be especially difficult. "Police often don't follow domestic violence procedures when it involves two women," she says. "Some cops think it is funny—it's a 'cat fight.'" Or worse, they will misjudge the situation and charge the wrong woman. "They go by stereotypes," she says. "They think the butch is always the abuser."

But police help is key. A woman with an abusive husband can quickly get an order of protection through Family Court, which does not require criminal charges against the abuser. Since New York City's domestic partnership program has no legal standing in Family Court, only lesbian couples that have legally adopted each other's children have access. For other lesbians, the order must be obtained through criminal court, meaning that a criminal case must be initiated against the ex-lover, says Nadya Rosen, a caseworker with Safe Homes' Lesbian/ Bi/Trans Women's Project. For a victim to get an order of protection, the batterer must commit an arrestable offense in the eyes of the law.

In Barbara's case, even the criminal courts were of little help. Though charged with attempted murder and convicted of assault, Barbara's ex-girlfriend was sentenced to only one day in jail. Barbara's advocates say the judge was somewhat sympathetic to the older woman and was unwilling to give her a long jail term.

"There is a sense that women do not believe women can be as violent as men," Rosen says. According to the Federal Bureau of Investigation, one in four heterosexual couples have abusive relationships. The Gay and Lesbian Anti-Violence Project (AVP) finds that gay couples aren't much different: They estimate one in five homosexual relationships is abusive.

Domestic Abuse in Lesbian Relationships

As with straight couples, domestic violence takes many forms: beatings, insults, rape, tyrannical jealousy. But gay couples are also vulnerable in more public ways. "For a lesbian, domestic violence can take the form of forced 'outing' by her partner," explains Diane Dolan-Soto, domestic violence program coordinator for the AVP. "If a woman is outed as a lesbian, she may lose her job or other necessary supports. If she is a mother, disclosing that she is a lesbian may mean risking the loss of her children."

Most traumatic of all, a lesbian victim of domestic violence who charges her partner with abuse may be accused of being a traitor to feminism or lesbianism. "There is definitely an element of not wanting to bring more stigma on our community," says Rosen. "By naming the violence, we are seen as reinforcing the stereotypes against 'out' women.

"A lot of us in the queer community are feminist," she adds. "It is hard, when you are political, to see your friend as a potential batterer. This traps women who are abused, when their community says they are lying."

To bring attention to the domestic violence problem in lesbian relationships, the Safe Homes staff and volunteers hold sensitivity trainings for other shelters throughout the city. They post fliers in popular women's hangouts in Brooklyn and Manhattan, and run a support group for lesbian, bisexual and transgender survivors of domestic violence—the only one of its kind in Brooklyn.

Serving Immigrant Arab Women

The experience that Safe Homes counselors had working with the close-knit lesbian community helped prepare them to begin work with some of Brooklyn's newest immigrants, Arabic-speaking women from North Africa and the Middle East. Some of the same issues—cultural isolation and insularity—are common to both groups, but Arab women have an additional difficulty: finding social workers that speak their language and understand the rules of Middle Eastern Islamic culture.

Safe Homes hired Jacqueline Jaber in 1998 to work with women in Brooklyn's growing Arab communities in Bay Ridge, Sunset Park and Park Slope, a population now topping 100,000 people. With just word of mouth and no advertising, Jaber's women now make up 8 percent of the 740 clients Safe Homes sees each year. Jaber, who speaks Arabic, works with a core group of 30 women, running support groups and translating for her clients as they try to work their way through the city bureaucracy.

Jaber, a gregarious Palestinian American with a hearty laugh, was raised in Brooklyn in a very religious Muslim family. "I was the eldest of 10 children and my mother was often sick," she says. "I grew up taking care of people." Jaber herself was in an arranged marriage that produced four children; she is now divorced.

Most of the women Jaber works with—including Palestinians, Moroccans, and Syrians—come from very traditional Muslim families. Some wear shara'a, the full-length gown and head scarf. Jaber must be able to negotiate dozens of different variations on nationality, class and cultural upbringing. "The Syrian women tend to be more educated," she says. "The Yemeni women often come from small villages and may speak only a local dialect of Arabic."

One of only two Arabic-speaking domestic violence counselors in New York City, Jaber is busy. "There are no city services for Arabic speakers," she says. So she also gets calls from non-Muslim Arab women, and has even helped the American-born wives of Middle Eastern men. "The problems with Arab men are the same [when they have] American wives—there is physical and economic abuse. They are controlling."

Providing Options for Battered Women

Jaber explains that her job isn't to change the women that come to her support group, but rather to provide them with options. "Many of these women do not see verbal abuse as abuse," she says. "I give them other points of view." She exposes her clients to liberal interpretations of the Koran, discussing their religion and how they view the violence in their lives. They must understand, Jaber says, "the Koran does not justify domestic violence."

For many of Jaber's clients, the biggest problem is that they don't know how to use New York City's support systems, which are nothing like the traditional ones they know from home. "If there is domestic violence in their native country, men from both families will meet with the local sheik to resolve the issue," she explains. "They do not have that support here." Much of Jaber's time is spent waiting in offices to translate for her clients, weathering impatient and harsh comments from caseworkers.

"The public assistance people ask why my clients dress in shara'a, why they have so many kids," she reports. "These are things they would never ask a black or Latino woman." Jaber says she has to answer even stupid questions politely to get the job done. "They ask me what I think about Iraq, or 'When you say Palestine, don't you mean Israel?' I don't have time to educate them. I have to get on to the next task."

One of her clients, Fatima, is a 33-year-old Palestinian woman with six children who now lives in Sunset Park. She had her first kid at age 15, and came to New York City at age 19. But her relationship with her husband, a store clerk, deteriorated after four or five years in New York. Soon, he abandoned the family, coming back regularly to beat up and yell at his wife. "I felt I had no options," Fatima says through a translator. "In our culture, you listen to your husband."

Jaber got Fatima the order of protection that keeps her violent husband away—Jaber reports that enlisting the cops is often very helpful, in part because many Arab men may be afraid of deportation. Jaber also suggests another reason: "Because they were raised under repressive regimes, they listen to men in uniform," she says with a chuckle.

She got Fatima on welfare, and Safe Homes is finding her a new apartment. "God willing, when the housing comes through, I will study English and, of course, get a job," says Fatima.

"Because I had no chance to be educated, I hope one of my children will go into higher education," she says. "I hope my daughters will have good reputations."

Both Yu and Jaber admit that dealing with the complexity of these particular brands of domestic violence is difficult, even exhausting. But both also report that the work can be rewarding, partly because they can see concrete results in women's lives. "I am proud of the work I do," says the pragmatic Jaber. "I am helping my community."

"We've painted a pretty dark picture of queer women being battered," admits Yu. "But they do survive. It is a testament to their strength."

WELFARE REFORM'S EFFECT ON BATTERED WOMEN

Jody Raphael

In 1996 Congress passed the Personal Responsibility and Work Opportunity Reconciliation Act, which authorized extensive reforms in the welfare system, including time limits on welfare benefits and work requirements for welfare recipients. In the following excerpt from her book *Saving Bernice: Battered Women, Welfare, and Poverty*, Jody Raphael examines the impact of this legislation on victims of domestic violence. She explains that when battered women attempt to better their lives through new jobs, their abusers typically try to sabotage their efforts by harassing them at work or accelerating the violence. Before requiring battered women to undertake job responsibilities, Raphael argues, welfare agencies should help them escape the abuse. Some welfare departments have already begun to hire on-site domestic violence advocates to screen victims and provide information about helpful resources, the author notes. Raphael is the director for research at the Center for Impact Research in Chicago, which endeavors to find new solutions to the problem of poverty.

In her 1998 memoir *Unafraid of the Dark*, the writer Rosemary Bray recounts her life in a family on welfare in Chicago. Bray's father was an abuser who frequently beat his wife and children severely. Bray writes that compliance with the provisions of the 1996 Federal welfare reform law would have resulted in more domestic violence for her mother and the children.

> There would have been no one to be with us after school, no one to intervene between me and my father's endless rages. And my mother's absence from home would have fueled my father's persistent jealousy. A man who could not tolerate his wife's grocery shopping would have been hard-pressed to accept her going to school eight hours a day with strangers. No, this plan for self-sufficiency would have meant the disintegration of my already fragile family life.

Jody Raphael, *Saving Bernice: Battered Women, Welfare, and Poverty*. Boston: Northeastern University Press, 2000. Copyright © 2000 by Jo Ann Raphael. All rights reserved. Reproduced by permission.

Had it been in place thirty years earlier, the new welfare bill would have taken my mother out of our home each day. Mama would have been required to attend a training program, in the hope that two years of training to work in food services or day care would serve as an adequate educational supplement to the third-grade education she had gotten a generation earlier. The four of us children, on the other hand, would have been left to fend for ourselves after school, in one of the worse neighborhoods of the United States.

Like Rosemary Bray's mother a generation ago, many women on welfare who are current victims of domestic violence may be unable to meet their state's work-related requirements without subjecting themselves and their children to serious danger of one kind or another.

Work Requirements Can Endanger Victims

In May 1998 the *Washington Post* reported a welfare-to-work story that had gone seriously wrong. Antoinette Goode, twenty-nine years of age, had completed a training course from which she emerged as the natural leader of the thirteen participating welfare recipients. Classmates reported that the stalking of her ex-boyfriend got worse and worse during the training. They observed him following Goode at lunch hour. After completing her training course Goode landed a job in 1997 with the federal Office of Personnel Management and subsequently won a promotion.

But Goode still had trouble with her children's father. At the end of May 1997 she was told that her ex-boyfriend was making threats against her. Frightened, she sought a new order of protection, which was denied because the threats were, according to the court intake worker, secondhand in nature. Antoinette Goode, a welfare-to-work success story, became a fatality statistic the next day. As her son and daughter watched in terror, she was stabbed to death as she walked home from a bus stop in Alexandria, Virginia.

Will abusers let women go to work knowing that if they do not, welfare benefits will be lost? In sixty-minute interviews with twenty-four respondents in her neighborhood study, Susan Lloyd found that some women decrease their work or fail to work because of partner interference, while others increase their work effort to reduce their reliance on husbands or boyfriends for economic security. . . .

Social Services Should Be the Priority

Anecdotal evidence from around the country suggests several different scenarios. Even when they are allowed to attend mandatory education, training, workfare programs, or employment, some women report that they receive harsh physical punishment at home. This kind of suffering is unconscionable. Better policy would have welfare departments assess domestic violence and provide services to help eliminate the abuse before women undertake labor market responsibilities. There are other instances in which, even though women are required to participate in work, their partners actively sabotage their activities or harass them on the job, eventually preventing their employment. Absent information, counseling, and support, many of these women cannot work out a way to extricate themselves into safety, and they may remain in the relationship but off welfare as a result. Still other battered women may never have thought about work and cannot even envision themselves out of the house in the wider world. For these women, the combination of violence and poverty also traps them in a situation that will certainly result in their remaining with their abuser and ultimately off welfare.

Even within the straitjacket of the time requirements of the new Temporary Assistance to Needy Families program (TANF), it is possible for welfare departments to sort out these cases and to attempt to provide needed help and resources. In response to the issue of domestic violence, welfare departments should be encouraged to provide as much individualized assistance as possible to help battered women make a safe transition to work.

The Family Violence Option

As welfare reform was initially being considered by the U.S. Senate in 1996, Senators Paul Wellstone (D, Minnesota) and Patty Murray (D, Washington) successfully amended the bill with a provision now known as the Family Violence Option. Under the Family Violence Option, if a state choosing to implement the option assesses domestic violence and refers a battered woman on welfare to domestic violence services, it may temporarily waive the twenty-four-month work requirement and the sixty-month lifetime limit on receipt of federal benefits, among others, and can escape federal financial penalties for failure to have the requisite number of women working each month. Although assessment of domestic violence within welfare offices is difficult at best and surely will result in many women choosing not to divulge their circumstances, the Family Violence Option gives battered women the chance to obtain needed help for the domestic violence before they tackle work issues. With the motto of "safety first" welfare departments can craft policies and procedures that can go a long way toward helping battered women rather than harming them.

Although many abusers control where their partner can go, most battered women say they are allowed to visit the welfare department office, even though the abuser may insist on driving them there and may sit in the waiting room or wait for them in the parking lot. Since most welfare departments do not allow the partners to accompany the women when they are called for their interview, the appointment provides a critical opportunity to provide information about domestic violence to these extremely isolated women.

[In 2000] one westside Chicago welfare office played a large role in one recipient's escape from domestic violence into safety. Upon request of the client's domestic violence advocate, the welfare case manager sent a letter to the victim, mandating an appointment and ordering the woman to bring her children along. As usual, her partner drove her to the welfare office. When she and the children were called in, by prearrangement a police car was ready in the back alley to transport them to a suburban domestic violence shelter. Eventually the woman settled permanently in this new community, found full-time employment, and now is off the welfare rolls.

In addition to meeting safety concerns, the Family Violence Option enables welfare departments to bring specialized domestic violence services to women on welfare, giving many of these women the opportunity to go through a recovery process for the first time, even as they may be attempting to engage in work activities. Many victims and survivors need to deal with a number of issues, including flashbacks, anger, or depression, with which a formal recovery process can greatly assist. Thus, one of the goals of welfare policy is to provide low-income girls and women the opportunity to recover fully from the trauma in a way that promotes their empowerment and gives them enough information so they can cope with the effects of the violence over the rest of their lives. Most low-income women struggle with these issues on their own, in isolation. Welfare reform is also the opportunity to bring needed interventions for children who have been traumatized by viewing the violence.

Other activities can be especially useful for battered women, including literacy training that rebuilds low basic skills and concomitant low social esteem, vocational exploration, and "work hardening," which consists of allowing a domestic violence victim to spend limited time in a work setting, with the time gradually increasing. Performing limited work activities allows the survivor to experience and develop her competency in a work setting or public arena.

Reluctant to Reveal Abuse

Early information about implementation of the Family Violence Option provides no real grounds for optimism about possible welfare department intervention. Although most states have chosen to implement the provisions of the Family Violence Option, as of the spring of 1999 few women appeared to be disclosing the domestic violence in their lives to their welfare workers. There is considerable doubt whether welfare case workers are actually telling women about the option, and it is unclear whether the women understand that they can so disclose without penalties and with full confidentiality. It is likely that many battered women simply will not entrust the disclosure of their abuse to a government worker.

For this reason, some welfare departments have, in some locations, hired or colocated trained domestic violence advocates in department offices who perform education and screening of domestic violence. Preliminary data indicate that women feel more comfortable confiding in a nongovernmental employee, and welfare workers also are relieved that they do not have to delve into personal matters with their clients. However, the expense connected with these schemes has generally prohibited their widespread expansion, although they hold out much hope of success. . . .

Helping Battered Women to Leave Their Abuser

Federal welfare reform now gives the states the flexibility to devise innovative approaches that could greatly assist battered women on welfare who may need onetime assistance with security deposits or the first month's rent, money for the purchase of a car to increase safety, or other more long-term assistance with transitional housing needs. Oregon's policy can serve as a model. Although there is a $350 maximum for any emergency, battered women can qualify for up to $1,200 with no payback by the participants. Funds can be used for housing and utility costs or relocation, for example. In November 1997, the state reports, it spent approximately $128,000 for emergency assistance for domestic violence victims for housing and utility costs, and $153,000 in December 1997. Many battered women need a small amount of financial assistance to relocate successfully. With a few exceptions, no state has really taken a good look at using welfare emergency assistance funds to facilitate and support women's escape plans.

It is also important to remember that for some women who have escaped the violence, getting on welfare may be a very good thing; without welfare benefits women are unable to leave a domestic violence shelter and establish a new home. Because many women continue to suffer from problems after they leave their abuser, including stalking, child custody battles, and severe physical and mental health problems, the victims may well need welfare for a period of time to stabilize their lives. The current political emphasis on welfare-to-work often obscures the role that welfare should and must play for battered women who are in the process of escaping their situation. To ensure that this safety net exists, welfare departments must be sensitive and flexible enough to take the needs of battered women into account. Welfare offices, for example, that direct all new applicants into job search or work search activities, even before approving their grant applications, are in danger of causing more damage to some battered women and their children. Some battered women will be able to start a job immediately, others may need a much longer period of healing, and still others may never be able to enter the workforce. Devising these individual plans is difficult in the current welfare reform environment that monolithically pushes applicants and recipients into jobs, but it can be done if there is the political will.

Insurance Discrimination Against Battered Women

Allison McCready

In the following selection, freelance writer Allison McCready discusses the problem of discrimination against battered women by insurance companies. As McCready explains, many insurance companies assume that victims of domestic violence are likely to be expensive to insure because of their increased risk of bodily injury and property loss at the hands of their abusers. Some insurance providers refuse to pay policyholder claims that involve domestic violence, she reports, while others deny coverage to battered women who apply for insurance policies. McCready contends that this type of discrimination harms battered women by prohibiting them from obtaining adequate insurance for themselves and their children; in fact, she states, a battered woman may choose to remain with her abusive partner because she fears losing her insurance if she leaves. According to the author, many states have begun to pass legislation protecting battered women from insurance discrimination, but more laws are needed to ensure that they are guaranteed adequate insurance coverage.

Kittis Bolduc did what she was supposed to do: she took herself and her children out of an abusive relationship and was in the process of getting a divorce. But even after she left that part of her life behind her, she became a victim once more, by an industry she thought would protect her.

"About 8:00, I got phone calls from Joe begging me to come back," Bolduc said in a taped interview with the Washington State Insurance Commissioner's office in September 1997. "He said, 'If you don't come back, I'll blow up the house.' This didn't really alarm me because he was always full of threats. He had threatened to do that before. He had threatened to do a lot of different things. So, after so many years of hearing threats you don't think in your wildest dreams—or nightmares—that this would ever occur to you, you know. 9:18 we received a phone call from my next door neighbor in

Allison McCready, "Perpetuating the Cycle of Violence: Insurance Discrimination Against Domestic Violence Victims," *National Business Women*, vol. 80, Spring 1999, p. 21. Copyright © 1999 by National Federation of Business and Professional Women's Clubs, Inc. Reproduced by permission.

hysterics that the house had blown up."

Bolduc's husband followed through with his threats and burned down their house. He was convicted of arson. But because of the intentional destruction of the house, and the fact that she and her husband were both listed on the policy, Safeco Insurance Co. refused to pay Bolduc's claim.

"Myself and my children are now double the victims because he chose to do this to us," Bolduc said. "We seem to be getting the punishment of someone else's criminal act."

Battered women already face overwhelming barriers when trying to get out of an abusive relationship: Some are financially dependent upon their abuser; others may fear retaliation by their partners against them or their children if they leave, or they may be so emotionally beaten down that they don't believe they deserve a better life. But they should not have to make a choice between staying in a destructive domestic situation and losing insurance coverage for themselves or their children.

Denied Coverage

Many insurance companies deny coverage to domestic violence victims by using evidence of abusive situations as part of the underwriting process: determining whom to cover and how much to charge for that coverage.

Some insurers classify domestic violence as a "lifestyle choice," like smoking, skydiving or riding a motorcycle. Others call it "career choice," like washing windows on a skyscraper, being a lion tamer, a professional boxer or a race car driver—choices for which an insurance company should not be responsible.

Statistics are sparse on how widespread insurance discrimination against battered women is because it often goes unreported. Insurance companies are not required by law to tell applicants why they have been denied coverage.

But one study done by the Insurance Commissioners of Pennsylvania in 1995 provides a glimpse at how pervasive the problem is. In the study, 24 percent of responding insurance companies said that they took domestic violence into account when determining to issue or renew insurance policies. Nearly 74 percent of responding life insurance companies said they looked for a history of domestic violence when deciding on new applicants; 65 percent of responding health insurance companies considered an applicant's abuse status when deciding on applications; and with accident insurers, the figure was 47 percent.

Nancy Durborow is the health projects coordinator at the Pennsylvania Coalition Against Domestic Violence, an advocacy and support services organization that has taken the lead on bringing this issue to the forefront of public consciousness. She became aware of the problem in 1993 when a woman came to her asking for help fighting a State Farm denial of her application for life insurance.

One of the problems is that consumers are not aware what kind of information they are giving insurers access to when they sign an application, Durborow said.

"We are all poor consumers," she said. "We don't read forms."

Medical Records May Reveal Abuse

When you sign a waiver to apply for insurance, you not only give an insurer authorization to check your medical records but authorization to get your information from one of the databases that many insurance companies belong to, according to Terry Fromson, managing attorney at the Women's Law Project, which provides legal aid to women fighting this type of insurance discrimination.

"The problem is that people don't understand the implications of signing these waivers," she said, "but if you don't sign it, you don't get insurance."

Also in 1993, a concerted effort was underway in the health care field to document cases of domestic violence.

"The insurance companies said, 'Tell the doctors not to document it or to white out the forms,'" Durborow said. "Of course, that would be a giant red flag. The doctors have not made the problem, the insurance companies have made the problem."

The logic for a woman caught in this Catch-22 is that if she hides her injuries from her health care provider, her insurance company will have no way of finding out she is in an abusive relationship, and they will not cancel her insurance. This only isolates a victim further from the people and institutions that can help her escape her violent situation, according to Durborow and Fromson.

Many in the insurance industry have denied that they are discriminating against victims of domestic violence, but have said that their decisions are sound insurance practices to prevent unnecessary loss.

"State Farm does not seek information from applicants or policyholders about whether they're involved in an abusive relationship; we have no reason to do so. However, information of that nature could appear in someone's medical records, claim information or be information volunteered by an individual," according to a State Farm media representative.

Domestic violence is a risk factor insurers must take into account in order to continue to offer affordable insurance, according to many in the industry. But insurers have produced no actuarial studies showing that domestic violence is a particular risk that changes the overall cost of insurance.

"There is insufficient data available to measure the costs associated with insuring victims of domestic violence," said State Farm spokeswoman Peg Echols at a 1995 Senate hearing.

Discrimination Against Service Providers

Discrimination on the basis of abuse extends to the advocates and services that exist to help women break free from their violent situations. The Colorado Coalition against Domestic Violence, a coalition of service providers that does no actual hands-on work with battered women, was denied insurance in 1996 by more than eight companies.

Director Laine Gibbs said it was because the coalition's name included the term "domestic violence," and the insurers told her they assumed the coalition was a shelter for battered women, which many companies won't insure because the women who live there run the risk of retaliation from their partners.

"We don't even serve victims," said Rachel Brown, community education and training coordinator for the coalition. "We do policy work and community education. We are a membership organization that helps train victims' advocates. We made that clear to the insurance companies, but that still didn't change anything.

"If we're getting discriminated against this much and we only have domestic violence in our name, imagine how women with domestic violence noted in their files are discriminated against." The coalition has never had an incidence where an abusive partner has shown up at the office, Brown said. Durborow said that in the 12 years she has worked at the Pennsylvania coalition only two violent incidents occurred.

"Not to say it's not there," she said, "but not to the extent the insurance companies portray it. The risk is not any greater than someone choosing your house to break into."

Laws Are Needed to Protect Victims

Currently, 31 states have laws in place that protect domestic violence victims from insurance discrimination and several more are considering legislation, but there's enormous variation in terms of what individual state's laws do, according to Fromson.

Victims' advocates are asking for too much from the insurance industry, said Don Cleasby, assistant general counsel for the National Association of Independent Insurers.

"Our problem with what they seem to be advocating is that it would prevent insurance companies from cost-based underwriting by identifying facts and data that show higher risk of loss to insurance companies," he said.

Bolduc's claim was not only denied, but, to add insult to injury, she was sued by her insurance company, Safeco. The judge ruled in favor of the insurer, but publicly chastised the company and urged the state legislature to take up the issue, according to Robert Harkins, deputy insurance commissioner for Washington state.

"Safeco didn't count on the public relations problem they had created," he said. "Even though they won, the ploy backfired. They realized they had taken a public relations bath and had created momentum to get the issue fixed."

Once on board, however, Safeco played a major role in helping get legislation prohibiting insurance discrimination against domestic violence victims passed in Washington state, he said.

But it shouldn't take bad publicity to activate a company's conscience. "Too often, it takes a situation to make a change," Harkins said. "It's not until they get burned that they get religious."

CHAPTER 4

BREAKING THE SILENCE: PERSONAL NARRATIVES OF ABUSE

My Private Nightmare

Cheryl Kravitz

Cheryl Kravitz is a freelance writer and the executive director of the National Conference for Community and Justice in Washington, D.C. In the following selection, Kravitz describes her experience as a middle-class victim of domestic violence. According to the author, she concealed the horror of her abuse under a veneer of professional success and domestic happiness. Like many middle-class women, Kravitz maintains, she had a particularly hard time admitting that she was being physically abused because she feared being socially stigmatized by her friends, colleagues, and family members. However, Kravitz reveals, it was only through the intervention of a concerned acquaintance that she found the strength to leave her abusive husband. After divorcing her husband and building a new life for herself, Kravitz continued to hide her abusive past from all but her closest friends—until she learned that her batterer had passed away. At that point, Kravitz began to share her story publicly in the hopes of helping other battered women escape their own abusive partners.

The nightmare would come in the hours before morning. It was always the same. I was crouched in the corner of my kitchen, hands over my head, eyes shut tight, gasping. In the background I could hear someone shouting obscenities while pummeling my back.

Sometimes I'd wake trembling, trying to get my bearings in the middle of the night. Fists clenched tight, my heart beating hard, I'd slowly take in my surroundings. *It was just a bad dream*, I'd tell myself. *You're safe. No one is going to hurt you.*

Years later, I can believe that I'm safe. But as one of the 4 million women physically abused every year by their husbands and boyfriends, it's taken the death of my tormentor for me to go public.

Many of those women are professionals, like myself, even elected officials, which I once was. Their abusers are clergy, doctors, psychologists, and executives, belying the stereotype that domestic violence is most prevalent among the poor or uneducated.

"Despite having greater resources available, it can be as difficult for

Cheryl Kravitz, "My Private Hell," *Washingtonian*, August 2000, p. 101. Copyright © 2000 by Washington Magazine, Inc. Reproduced by permission.

middle-class women to leave a batterer as it is for poor women," says Chevy Chase psychiatrist Susan Fiester. "They feel humiliated and believe they will be stigmatized once the community finds out about the situation."

But going public gives another battered woman a chance to see that she's not alone. So it's a gamble worth taking for me. . . .

Meeting Larry

In my mid-twenties, I'd finally reached a point where I felt that life was good. I had become a mother at 17, and my daughter and I had weathered a lot together, but by 1975 our lives were placid.

We lived in Chicago in an apartment with a view of Lake Michigan. I was editor of the community newspaper, the *Hyde Park Herald*, and my daughter attended third grade at a neighborhood school. My parents helped with my daughter, and my friends formed a tight circle of support, albeit one that concentrated mostly on assisting each other with dating advice.

That spring I enrolled my daughter in day camp at the Jewish Community Center. Soon after, a staff member there asked if I'd consider writing an article about the new executive director, considered a rising star in the community. Besides, she said, he was single.

After quick consultations with my friends, we decided this was the perfect opportunity. I could find out everything I wanted to know about a potential suitor in a legitimate interview.

Looking back, I can see why the incentives to settle down were so strong. My parents disowned me when I became pregnant at 16. We had no contact for three years, and when the reconciliation finally occurred I swore I would do whatever I could to become a "good girl" again.

By the time 1975 rolled around, the relationship with my parents was smooth. The only thing missing in my life was the companionship of a man. In my mind, this man, through his religion, education, occupation, wit, and style, would be the acknowledgment to the outside world that I was approved.

Enter Larry.

The day of the interview I primped for an hour, double-checking my questions. By the interview's end, I was smitten with this Yale-educated man. That afternoon he called and asked if I'd like to go to a Smothers Brothers benefit that weekend.

The next few months were an avalanche of lavish dinners, weekend trips, and beautiful gifts. He won a high approval rating from my family and friends. By the time the engagement announcement ran on page three of the *Herald*, we were considered a hot couple in Hyde Park.

There were just a few things that I chose to ignore.

It didn't occur to me to question why Larry neglected to tell me that he had been married twice before or that his tendency to disappear into another room several times a night was a chance for him to down a couple glasses of vodka.

I felt no need to respond when his father, as gently as he could, suggested I might wait a bit before making this commitment, but didn't tell me why that might be wise. The day before the wedding Larry was upset that I was on the phone for a long time with my best friend. I chalked it up to nerves when he found an antique cup my friend had given me and smashed it against a wall.

A Gradual Shift in Power

By winter of 1977, blinded by my new standing in the community, I didn't notice that there had been a shift in power between Larry and me.

With Larry's encouragement, I'd left my beloved newspaper job and, at twice the salary, went to work for a local hospital as communications director. Because I'd never had to manage this much money I began turning my paycheck over to him, receiving an allowance in return.

I barely noticed that my circle of friends had dwindled since I was increasingly unavailable. Even lunches out became hard because my allowance was not large, and every penny needed to be accounted for at the end of the week.

My parents took care of my daughter every weekend because Larry felt we needed time alone to do things as a married couple. In our new apartment, amid the nice furniture and lovely wedding gifts, my attention wasn't focused on reality. We weren't going out at all. The weekends were spent in the apartment, with me trying to read and him drinking vodka openly now, constantly complaining about his job.

In the spring of 1978 the problems at his job were overwhelming. Larry had alienated people by his argumentative posturing at meetings, and many of the community leaders with whom I had been close were calling for his ouster. I felt torn between my duty as a wife and my knowledge that these were good, decent people who were seldom wrong.

Finally, one of Larry's mentors suggested the time was right to leave. There was a job opening in Tulsa, Oklahoma, to head the Jewish Community Center there. Within a few weeks, the job was his.

Leaving Home

We were scheduled to leave at the end of August. Larry had lived in five cities. I'd never lived anywhere but Chicago. The farewells were wrenching.

Our car headed south toward unfamiliar Tulsa and away from the city and the life I'd always known. No friends, no job, separated from my family, with no money of my own, I went to Oklahoma. My isolation was now complete.

Larry was elated. We bought a beautiful home and, with my 11-year-old daughter in an excellent school, the halcyon days were back. My urge to go back to work was met with approval and within two months I'd found a perfect position, with the Red Cross.

By the time I turned 30 the problems in Chicago were a distant memory. My work was exciting and my daughter was thriving. I'd made new friends and was freelance writing for a daily newspaper.

It's hard to remember when the ground shifted. Once again the changes were slow and subtle. It might have been when I resisted handing over my paycheck for the first time or when the phone kept ringing because I'd won an award for my newspaper column.

The pouting and drinking seemed to increase incrementally with any outside recognition that I received.

Such jealousy and possessiveness are common traits of batterers, who become overinvolved in their partner's life in order to feel secure themselves, according to Lenore E. Walker in her landmark book, *The Battered Woman*. Also not unusual was Larry's insistence that I turn over all money to him.

"The use of economic deprivation as a coercive technique results in bargaining and tradeoffs," Walker writes. "Not only is the woman deprived economically, but also she is emotionally deprived as an adult."

So I started withholding information, sharing only those items that I knew would gain Larry's approval. A raise would do that. Or another freelance job. Once again I signed my checks over to him.

We'd been in Tulsa for two years when the complaints about his job started. "They" didn't appreciate him; he was much too good for this; he was tired of constant meetings and decisions. And I was no help. I was more concerned about my own job and my daughter than about his troubles. The cleanliness of the house wasn't up to his standards. The dogs were a nuisance. I wasn't making enough money. I looked ugly. On and on and on.

The Abuse Begins

I can't remember the first time Larry hit me. I've blocked that memory. I know by the summer of 1981 his behavior was bizarre. Somehow he was able to function at his job, but when he came home it was a different story.

The minute he arrived he would open a half-gallon bottle of vodka and start to drink. He then began a ritual of going through the house to see what was wrong. The infringements could be anything from a spoon out of place to an unmade bed. The worst were when one of the dogs had an accident or my daughter failed to put away her clothes.

At first the aggression was confined to pushing and verbal abuse. If the plates weren't lined up in the dishwasher just right, he might grab my arm and propel me into the wall. Or, if I saved my allowance and bought a new dress, he would complain about how badly it fit or how ghastly the color was. Nothing I did was right.

Logic says that at this point anyone with any self-respect would have left, but my self-respect was in shreds, and I felt there were no options. I couldn't go back to Chicago. In my mind that would be admitting defeat, hurting my parents again. I barely had contact with any of my old friends and I felt my return would be shameful. It was unthinkable to tell Larry's family, and to "come out" in Tulsa would have been impossible. I felt I was too well known, too respected to let anyone in on my secret.

My reaction fit author Lenore Walker's description of "learned help-lessness." The battered woman, she says, presents a passive face to the world, while somehow finding the strength at home to manipulate her environment enough to prevent further violence or being killed.

In my case, the "incidents" were spaced far enough apart that a pattern hadn't emerged. I could excuse it by blaming his moods on stress. Periodically he would become maniacally nice, sending flow-ers, buying extravagant gifts, and, in one rare instance, letting me keep my paycheck.

And so I stayed.

Around this time it became apparent that Larry was going to lose his job. Again, it was his confrontational nature—arguing with volun-teers, posturing in meetings, fighting with his boss. So the only place he felt totally in control was at home.

One day I came home from work to find everything taken out of the kitchen cabinets and scattered over the foyer. I was told that because I was such a poor housekeeper it might be easier to keep everything on the floor, and that nothing should be returned to the cabinets. He delighted in lining up his empty vodka bottles on the floor of his study, one of the rooms in the house that were off-limits to me.

My daughter, meanwhile, was in the throes of a difficult adoles-cence. We didn't talk about what was happening to me or about what she heard or saw. Once an outgoing and sunny child, she now was increasingly sullen and withdrawn. She was hanging out with a wild crowd, and I didn't have the energy to help her.

The abuses seemed to expand with my success. In 1982 I was cited nationally by the Red Cross for my work, and I traveled to Atlanta to receive an award, leaving my daughter with friends.

Larry seemed contrite when I arrived home. He handed me the newspaper. The Tulsa dailies listed all arrests for drunk driving, and there was his name.

He lost his job immediately. And I came to learn that the previous abuse was a rehearsal for what was to come.

The Abuse Escalates

The next two years have blended together into a bad memory. I was no longer allowed to sleep in the bedroom; Larry told me I was so unattractive that I didn't deserve to be in the same bed with him. My choices were the kitchen floor with the dogs, the front hall surrounded by the cans and dishes, or with my daughter.

He threatened to kill my favorite dog and make me watch while he did it. His pushes escalated to slaps, and then punches. He was careful not to hit my face. To cover the black-and-blue marks, I wore long sleeves and long pants, even in the heat of a Tulsa summer.

By 1984 I was in a deep depression, but had become so adept at hiding my wounds and my psychological pain that no one guessed what was going on at home.

I was like many battered women, as described by Lenore Walker: socially isolated, humiliated, and believing that if I did not obey orders I would be seriously harmed. The battered woman might not reach out for help because she sees her abuser as more powerful than anyone who might attempt to save her.

Middle-class women, especially, think no one will help them, Walker says, because no one wants to believe that men regarded as pillars of the community are capable of this behavior.

That year two important things happened: I was selected to be a member of Leadership Tulsa, part of the same movement as Leadership Washington, and I was recruited to run for the school board. Without any sound reasoning, given my personal circumstances, I chose to do both.

Leadership Tulsa had a graduation requirement: You had to serve for a year with a nonprofit organization—one with a mission different from that of any other group you had worked with in the past. I was assigned to help run the capital campaign for Domestic Violence Intervention Services—never revealing my own situation.

The group that asked me to run for the school board was headed by the mother of one of my daughter's friends. It was the friend whose house I insisted my daughter stay at when I went out of town for work, or sensed an incident was imminent.

The election and my work with the domestic-violence group took on lives of their own. When I was out making speeches, or helping raise money for the new shelter, I almost felt like myself again. The election [was] tough, but I won. And then the ground shifted again.

One night Larry started a new game. He would turn off all the lights and hide. I would sit in the kitchen, waiting for him to emerge. Some nights nothing happened. Other times the battering took new turns. He took the dog's flea spray and held it on my face in an unrelenting stream. He kept a bat under his bed and threatened to bash my head in. Instead, he shattered all the wedding crystal.

When he'd knock me to the ground, my new way of coping was to pretend I was wrapped in yards and yards of cotton, so I couldn't feel the blows. I also had a fantasy of sending my soul to the ceiling so the only thing he was breaking was my body, not my spirit.

I would look in the mirror after a beating and I couldn't seem to make out my face. I was that detached from myself.

A Turning Point

March 10, 1985, was one of those yellowish-gray Oklahoma days that portend a storm. The night before had been particularly hard, and I knew the night to come was going to be no different. I called the mother of my daughter's friend and asked if my child could spend the night there.

This time she didn't automatically say yes. She started questioning me: Why wasn't I letting anyone into the house? How come I was always wearing long sleeves? Why was I always so secretive about Larry? And then she asked the question. "You're being hurt, aren't you? Can I help you?"

In that moment I knew I had to let her into my life, at least a little. I told her I was in a bad situation that was getting worse. I promised that if she let my daughter spend the night at her house I would sleep in my daughter's room with a portable phone nearby.

When I arrived home from work Larry was drunk. I turned on the oven to heat a frozen dinner.

Larry grabbed me by the hair and threw me to the kitchen floor, kicking me as I tried to crawl away. Crouched in the corner, hands over my head, eyes shut tight, gasping, I prayed for my life. I prayed that there would be a sign that someone cared about me. Larry wouldn't let up, finally grabbing my arms and sticking them in the oven, burning them on the rack.

I fell screaming. He kicked me again, stormed into the bedroom, and soon passed out from the alcohol. I found my way to the bathroom and put salve on my arms. So drained I could barely move, I crawled into the guest room and fell asleep on the floor.

A few hours later I heard pounding on the front door. It was a police officer and the mother of my daughter's friend. She had tried to call, but I hadn't heard the phone. She cared. Suddenly, I cared too. I walked outside and into her waiting arms.

We drove to her house, and I spent the next few hours talking about everything that had been hidden for so long. My daughter joined us, visibly relieved. Although Larry had never touched her physically, her mental anguish was palpable.

Our friends said we could stay with them for a while. They lent us money until I received my next paycheck, the first one I could use to finally establish my own checking account.

I called the director of Domestic Violence Intervention Services and told her everything. She told me she had suspected something from watching my behavior and other clues. She contacted the DVIS support network and in no time I had an attorney and a therapist. The more people who knew, the less alone I felt. My embarrassment began to fade as I learned more about abuse.

The divorce was not easy. Because I'd left in the middle of the night with only the clothes on my back, we needed a court order to get back in the house so I could retrieve our clothing, some furniture, and our dog. I was even able to see the humor in my friend's shock at the pots, pans, and food in the front hallway. She thought Larry had emptied the cabinets earlier that day in a fit of pique.

The attorney filed a protective order. Larry was required to stay away from my daughter and me. I didn't want a long court battle, so I decided not to file assault charges against him.

I called my parents and told them what had happened, omitting the worst parts. They were not surprised. After all this time, my mother said she always thought Larry was a bit odd. My father agreed. So much for my concern about their anger.

Starting Over

My daughter and I found a small apartment and moved in within the month. It was the first time in years that we were able to live in a place that reflected who we were. The house had always been dark because Larry insisted that the curtains remain closed. Now we opened every window and let the sunshine inside.

Within months the divorce was final. On that day, I spent the time with a friend making a picture frame for a print for our apartment. I wanted to do something I'd never tried before and looked for the type of activity Larry would say I could never accomplish. The framed poster hangs in my living room today.

My daughter had graduated from high school that June and decided to attend the University of Arizona. She wanted to become a social worker with a special interest in working with abused children—a goal she has accomplished.

The following spring, in 1986, I was offered a position at Red Cross headquarters in Washington. When the plane circled the city, I knew I was coming home.

I thought I had left behind the drama of domestic abuse. Yet while I was waiting in a real-estate office one day, my gaze fell on the cover of that month's *Washingtonian*. It was a photograph of an attractive woman looking straight at me. Her name was Charlotte Fedders, and she told the story of her marriage to a powerful lawyer, her country-club membership and house in Potomac, and how her husband often beat her.

I couldn't believe there was another woman in circumstances like mine—a life filled with outward appearances of success but tortured by abuse. Reading her story confirmed for me that I had done the right thing when I left my husband.

The year after I arrived in Washington, I met my soul mate. We just celebrated our 11th wedding anniversary and have a seven-year-old daughter we adore. My husband is witty and smart, and in a million years I couldn't imagine him raising his hand to hit me.

My life in Tulsa seemed a distant memory as my life in Washington blossomed. I became executive director of the National Conference for Community and Justice, where my work centers on fighting prejudice of all kinds.

In my job, I meet with community groups and talk about the roles bias and bigotry play in our lives and what we can do to change our behavior. In one exercise I do with groups, we talk about the "real person behind the face." But for the longest time I wasn't able to reveal that part of my "real person" is someone who is a former battered wife.

The biggest change for me took place at home. Like a prisoner of war must feel upon his or her release, I felt that every day is a gift. In the first months after my new marriage, it felt like a victory to wake up with my husband beside me. Putting a pan in the cabinet, buying a new dress, not accounting for my paycheck—it was like being granted a second chance at life.

And because I wasn't on edge all the time, I found Washington to be a warm, welcoming place to live and work. When we adopted our daughter, our circle of friends grew even larger. The best part is being free to invite these people into our home—something I never dared do during my first marriage.

Going Public

Life was good. Except I wasn't sure where Larry was. Every day I feared that he would reappear and beat me one last time.

I figured he knew I had moved here and it was just a matter of time before he tracked me down. I had recurring nightmares, and despite my husband's assurances that everything was fine, I kept waiting for the other shoe to drop. Every time I'd read a story about domestic violence I'd shudder in fear. During the O.J. Simpson trial I relived my own terror daily.

One night [in 1999] I went on the Internet to look for him. There was a listing for a Larry with his last name in his hometown of Kansas City. He was living there with his wife. And according to the listing, her name was Cheryl.

I was frightened. I called a friend who had access to Lexis-Nexis and was able to do a comprehensive search. He called back and asked me to sit down: "You're not going to believe this—he's dead."

Larry had died in 1995. In some ways it was his final strike at me. I'd spent the past few years living in fear of him, and he wasn't even alive. Because I didn't stay in touch with his parents or his brother, and we didn't have mutual friends, there hadn't been any way for me to hear about his death.

I took a deep breath and called my daughter with the news.

Then I did what years ago would have been unthinkable. I decided to "come out." I wrote an article for the *Washington Post* about being battered. I briefly told my story and made the point that the signs that a person is being abused are apparent if you're willing to see them. And then you have to be ready to act.

I hear from women in this city who have been, or are being, abused. I've been in a high-level business meeting and had a note passed to me from someone who once suffered physical abuse. I've been involved in Leadership Washington and have heard from fellow community leaders who have had the same experience of abuse.

They are like me. Many are middle-class. They are considered bright and warm and generous. And when they read that they were not alone in their confusion, pain, and humiliation, they took a leap of faith and began to tell their stories.

My hope is that every person who is battered will somehow find the strength to walk out of their house of horrors. On the other side of the door, the welcoming arms of a compassionate community will be waiting.

THE LUCKIEST DAY OF HIS LIFE

Bill Ibelle

In the following selection, Bill Ibelle interviews a former batterer, Donald, and his wife. Donald describes the five years during which he abused his wife, his arrest, his experiences in the treatment program, and the changes he has made in his relationship with his wife. Donald's wife also tells Ibelle what it was like to be a victim of abuse. Donald explains that he learned in treatment that batterers must learn to take full responsibility for the beatings rather than finding someone else to blame. Despite the poor prognosis for most batterers, Donald believes that his arrest and his subsequent participation in a batterer treatment program has resulted in a lasting change in his behavior. Ibelle is a features editor at *Lawyers Weekly USA*, a newspaper that covers legal issues.

Donald beat his wife.

He gave her black eyes, silenced her with looks of impending rage, insisted on controlling her every move, and ensured all this remained a secret by isolating her from friends and family.

He was, in short, a batterer: one of a group of men who cause more injuries to women in this country than car accidents, muggings and rapes combined, according to statistics compiled by the National Women's Health Resource Center.

The prognosis for batterers is not good. Even the best estimates put the success rate at around 40 percent, and success is defined as refraining from violence for just one year.

But unlike most batterers, Donald changed his ways in 1994 after he was arrested, sent to jail and ordered to enroll in a batterers' treatment program at the Community Center for Non-Violence in New Bedford, Massachusetts.

Today Donald and his wife agree that the violence has stopped, their relationship has improved and their two small daughters are growing up in a much healthier environment.

Donald—who agreed to be interviewed under the condition that his last name not be used—credits the police, the courts and the treatment program for this dramatic turn of events.

"I'm glad the law finally stopped me," he said. "They locked me up for six months and it changed my life. If I hadn't stopped when I did, it only would have gotten worse. Sooner or later she would have gotten really hurt. I really believe that."

Five Years of Abuse

Donald said he abused his wife throughout their five-year marriage.

It could start with anything—a minor offhand comment from his wife, a late dinner; sometimes he would be angry because they didn't have money to pay the rent.

"When he got like that, I knew there was a beating coming on," said his wife, who asked that her name not be used. "At times I'd be so scared I'd be shaking inside. Sometimes I'd think, maybe I should just kill myself before he gets home—just to get it over with."

According to Donald, the beatings, the verbal abuse and the intimidation were all about control.

"It was like having a new toy," he said. "I had the buttons and I could make her do whatever I wanted. I was trying to intimidate her. I wanted to control her for the simple reason that I knew I could do it. It made me feel powerful."

Whenever Donald's wife left the house, he gave her a specific amount of time to complete the excursion. If she was late, he beat her. But most of the time he didn't have to, because the mere threat of abuse was enough to make his wife toe the line.

"I'd be at my girlfriend's looking at my watch the whole time because I knew that if I was late, I'd get hit," she said.

The longer the abuse continued, the tighter the controls became.

"Pretty soon, I didn't have any friends," she said. "I'd be invited to parties but I always made up an excuse. I never brought anyone to my house. He even stopped me from talking to anyone in the family because he was scared I'd tell someone."

While the actual physical abuse was sporadic, the psychological abuse was relentless. Whenever Donald drank, his rage bubbled dangerously close to the surface. This alone was enough to make his wife cower in his presence.

"He'd growl like a monster," she said. "I was too terrified to get help because I figured I'd get killed when I got back. So I never told anyone he hit me."

Like many batterers, Donald was highly manipulative and had a keen sense of when he had pushed his wife too far. Whenever she was about to leave, he would apologize, shower her with presents and tell her how much he loved her and the kids.

"I'd con my way right out of it," he said. "I conned everyone. At work I was just a fun-loving guy. No one would have ever suspected the way I was at home. It felt good. But it finally caught up with me."

The first two times Donald was arrested, his wife refused to cooperate with the police so he was charged with disorderly conduct, taken into protective custody and released the next day.

Meanwhile, the abuse escalated. Not only was Donald's wife in mortal danger, so was Donald.

"I thought 'I'll just kill him. That will solve everything. I'll kill him and then go right to the police and tell them what I'd done and why I did it,'" she said.

The Arrest

Luckily for both of them, the law stepped in before it was too late. While Donald's wife was out getting a pizza for the family, she ran into some police officers she knew from working the night shift at a local doughnut shop. The officers saw the bruises on her face and convinced her to give a statement about the abuse at home. The bruises and her story were all the police needed to take action.

When Donald's wife arrived home with the pizza, the police were already leading him out of the house in handcuffs and the kids were asking where the men were taking daddy.

Donald was sentenced to 1½ years in jail. He was released after six months in an intensive alcohol program under the condition that he enroll immediately in batterers treatment.

Unlike many others, Donald entered the Community Center for Non-Violence determined to turn his life around. He was horrified that his daughter watched the police haul him off to jail in handcuffs and that he missed his other daughter's first birthday. In spite of the years of abuse, his wife stuck by him even after his arrest. That, too, filled him with remorse.

"She had every right to leave," he said. "I put her through hell. I assumed it was over but she came to visit me every week. That made me feel bad. I owe her for that. I swore that will never happen again."

During the first portion of the batterers program, group members are confronted with their deeds. The goal is to make them accept responsibility for their actions—to stop blaming their partners, booze, their temper.

"They continually stressed that it was our behavior that got us into this situation," said Donald. "It's not what she did or what she said—we had to take responsibility for our actions."

Taking full responsibility for the beatings is a key hurdle to graduating to the second part of the treatment program. Because he had already admitted his problem, this took Donald only four weeks.

But most men arrive at batterers treatment convinced that someone else is to blame—their partner, the police, the judge. For these men, it can take several months to get past the first stage of treatment. Some never make it and wind up back in jail.

During the second portion of the treatment program, men focus more on finding the source of their violence and ways to manage their rage. They discuss attitudes toward women and their demand for total control. They explore their childhood, the way their parents treated each other and the attitudes and communication patterns they learned in childhood.

"When I first got into the program I didn't know what to expect," said Donald. "I couldn't imagine sharing my problems with a bunch of strangers. But this is something I needed for myself and my kids. I was there to get the help. I wasn't going to let this happen to my kids again."

As the men explore these issues, they also learn relaxation techniques, ways to recognize the warning signs of building rage and ways to diffuse that rage. They learn better ways of communicating with their partner to avoid unnecessary battles and develop a richer relationship.

Learning the Victim's Perspective

Half way through the program, clients at the local women's center discuss domestic violence from the victim's perspective.

"It was terrifying—especially hearing about the children," said Donald. "She told us stories that made my skin crawl. They made me take a good look at myself. It put a real bad guilt on me."

Donald has a tough time putting into words what he got out of the program. He says he learned that his wife is a human being too. That may not sound like much, but experts say that this is a huge step for many batterers.

"I learned that it takes two people to make a relationship," he said. "I didn't let her do anything. I said it was all a man's job. Now I realize I have a partner in this marriage and I better learn to talk."

Donald's wife agrees their relationship has improved. She is included in the decision making and has more personal freedom. Since Donald completed the program, she has enrolled at Fisher College to become a medical assistant.

"I never would have allowed that before," said Donald. "I was the working man and I wanted her home getting supper on the table."

He has stopped drinking and learned to control his temper. When he feels himself losing control, he leaves the situation and comes back later to discuss the disagreement. When he talks with his wife, he actually listens to her.

As a result, the entire family's life has improved dramatically.

In the first five years of their marriage, they lived in six different apartments because Donald kept losing jobs and falling behind in the rent.

Since he completed the alcohol program, Donald has found a lucrative welding job, bought a house and a new car.

"Since all this happened I've changed a lot," he said. "I don't think I'll ever relapse. I know I'd lose everything—this house, these kids, her—everything. I still have a lot to prove to a lot of people. But the most important people I've got to prove it to are me and her. I'm not going to blow it this time."

He paused.

"I just hope it stops here. I don't want my daughters to grow up and get married and end up going through this same thing."

AN ACT OF SELF-DEFENSE

Alexandra Marks

Alexandra Marks is a staff writer for the *Christian Science Monitor*. In the following selection, she describes the experiences of Linda White, who was physically and psychologically abused by her boyfriend. As Marks explains, White broke off the relationship and sought help from the police and the courts, but her efforts only angered her abuser, who became increasingly violent. One day in 1989, after her abuser held a loaded gun to her head, White shot and killed him. She was convicted of second-degree murder and served more than twelve years in prison before being granted clemency by the governor of New York. White is now determined to use her experience to help other women who are still trapped in abusive relationships, the author relates.

Linda White turns her wrist over and touches the half a dozen or so thin scars on her forearm.

"You can still see them," she says, sounding almost surprised. "That was from one of the times he tied me up. He also cut me."

"He" is her former boyfriend. A man named John Strouble. In 1989, after a year of severe psychological and physical abuse, Ms. White fatally shot him.

She used his gun—one that she says he routinely shot out the window, then put to her head to let her know he could and would kill her.

White pleaded self-defense, but was convicted of second-degree murder and was given 17 years to life in prison. But after serving more than 12 years, she has been granted clemency by New York Gov. George Pataki.

Like all stories about battering and abuse, hers is complicated. But it also provides a lens to illustrate the strides made as well as the setbacks within the nation's criminal justice system in its dealings with battered women over the past 20 years.

There are now hundreds of domestic-abuse hot lines and battered-women's shelters. And there have been major reforms in the criminal justice system, from special training for police to the establishment of protection orders in the courts.

Alexandra Marks, "One Woman's Story About Domestic Abuse and Justice," *Christian Science Monitor*, vol. 95, January 27, 2003, p. 4. Copyright © 2003 by The Christian Science Publishing Society. All rights reserved. Reproduced by permission.

But experts say that even as those advances raised public awareness and helped thousands of individuals, their effectiveness remains spotty. And they've also had an unintended consequence: Experts say they've fueled a backlash that makes it more difficult for women like Linda White to successfully plead self-defense.

"People had hoped that all of the interventions would make police and prosecutors and judges more savvy about what happens to battered women in violent relationships," says Holly Maguigan, a professor of political law at New York University. "But it is still very hard for people to understand that a woman like Linda White who uses serious force may be reasonable and justified."

During the 1990s, reported domestic violence dropped, although not as precipitously as the overall crime rate. In fact, Justice Department statistics tell a surprising story about the impact of increased awareness and services: They may have saved more men's lives than women's.

In 1976, according to the Bureau of Justice Statistics, 1,357 men and 1,600 women were killed in what the FBI refers to as "intimate partner" homicides. By 1999, the number of men killed by spouses, former spouses, or girlfriends had declined to 424, a drop of 69 percent. But the number of women killed decreased to only 1,218, a drop of just 24 percent.

Experts believe that's because shelters and hot lines have given women with access to them the ability to leave before they reach a breaking point. But abusive men do not have similar resources at their disposal. And studies still show that it is when an abused woman decides to leave that her batterer is the most likely to kill her.

"Women tend to kill when they're defending themselves, and the increased services have helped give women with access to them other options," says Sue Osthoff, director of the National Clearinghouse for the Defense of Battered Women. "But men haven't really changed that much."

A Characteristic Case

Linda White is an example of a woman who tried to leave but says she couldn't for fear of her life. Her interactions with the social-service system also exemplify the advances, as well as the huge gaps that remain in providing help to battered women.

To start, she says she'd never heard of a "battered woman" syndrome when she met Mr. Strouble. She was in her early 40s. She had raised three children, and after her mother died, she took in four much younger siblings, including a retarded brother.

White lived in a housing project in Queens. She worked her whole life as a cashier and clerk to support her family, except for a brief period in the early 1970s, when she went on welfare after taking in her siblings.

"Linda White was in 99.9 percent of her life an exemplary person, except in this one moment when she needed to defend herself. She's already paid a high price for that," says Julie Blackman, a social psychologist and expert on battered women.

According to White and court records, the abuse started a few months after she and Strouble met. She mentioned that he'd forgotten her birthday. His response was to slap her. His behavior became increasingly erratic. She suspected he was using drugs and asked him to leave her apartment. That started the cycle of beatings.

She changed her locks four times to try to keep him out. She called the police, who walked him around the block to "cool him off." She got a protection order forbidding him to come near her. He tore it up. Indeed, each effort to keep him away only enraged him and intensified the abuse.

One day, Strouble again played his game of Russian roulette with her, but instead of putting the gun away in his toolbox as he usually did, he left it on the bedside table. She walked out of the bathroom, saw it, picked it up, and shot him.

At her trial, prosecutors contended she was a coldblooded, jealous woman who killed Strouble because he was talking to a previous girlfriend with whom he had a child. The judge, who called her relationship with Strouble "stormy," also doubted some of the more horrific instances of abuse because she didn't seek medical attention.

Domestic-abuse experts say that characterization reflects a lack of understanding of battered woman's syndrome. "I would be shocked today to find anyone convicted of murder in a similar case," says Sara Bennett, White's appellate attorney.

Ms. Bennett provided a list of similar cases from the past decade where women, many of whom endured less severe abuse, were convicted of manslaughter and given shorter sentences.

Yet other experts in domestic abuse, like Professor Maguigan, contend that abused women's success in pleading self-defense is often dependent on whether they get attorneys and experts who are experienced in dealing with the special challenges of their cases. That such expertise exists is part of the progress that's been made.

The judge in White's case did not oppose her clemency request, as he did previously. The Queens' district attorney also didn't object—although Warren Silverman, the DA who tried the case, still believes she was an angry spurned lover, not an abused woman. "I just didn't think she was truly a battered woman," says Mr. Silverman. "But let's assume she is a battered woman. It doesn't give her the right to kill her batterer."

As for White herself, the clemency granted by Governor Pataki comes as a great gift and a relief. She's determined to put her experience to work for the good of others.

"I want to work with women who are going through it now. I can talk to them and tell them what to do: 'Leave, no matter what. You got to go,'" she says.

"I didn't see that then, but I see it now."

My Experience as a Batterer

Duane Minard, as told to Tara McKelvey

Duane Minard, a former abusive husband, details his long road to recovery in the following article. Minard explains that he physically abused his first two wives until those marriages ended in divorce. His third wife, however, filed a police report against him after enduring a brutal beating at his hands. It was at this point, Minard confesses, that he realized he had a serious problem and made a commitment to end his abusive behavior. He entered a batterers' intervention program and read books on domestic violence, which helped him understand how he had learned violent behavior from his abusive father during his childhood. Minard relates that his wife agreed to a reconciliation on strict terms, including a signed contract requiring an end to his violent behavior. The couple has also founded an outreach organization for victims of domestic violence, and Minard gives talks on domestic violence to groups of men. Based in Washington, D.C., writer Tara McKelvey is a frequent contributor to *Marie Claire*.

I never imagined I could hurt a woman—until I did. I then spent years telling myself she deserved it. The first time I was 20, and my 18-year-old bride, Cheryl, slept with my best friend. When I found out, I felt so betrayed that I called her every demeaning name I knew. For seven years, I berated her, slapped her, and pushed her around. By attacking Cheryl, I felt like I had control over her—and myself. She'd had an affair, I'd tell myself, and now I had to keep her in line.

When Cheryl left me, I didn't feel guilty or responsible. Instead I thought, next time, I'll marry a woman who is strong enough to take it.

I met my second wife, Pam, at work, where I was a police detective and she was a sheriff's aide. She had an appealing combination of toughness and compassion. "Watch your head getting in the car," she'd say to the perpetrators we arrested. And yet, whenever one of these guys talked back to her, she put him in his place.

Pam and I got married—and that's when we started arguing. Our fights became physical: I'd shove her, she'd shove me back. I'd pull

Tara McKelvey, "Why I Beat Her," *Marie Claire*, vol. 10, October 2003, p. 139. Copyright © 2003 by Hearst Brand Development. Reproduced by permission.

her hair, she'd pull mine. Aggression was normal to us; we had both grown up with it. We continued to mistreat each other for 10 years, until we finally agreed to divorce.

When I met Cesaria in 1999, I thought, now this is a woman I could love. Sure, I had a history of losing my temper, but that was over. After all, I told myself, I wasn't the problem—it was the women I'd married. My first wife had cheated; my second wife had provoked me. There would be no reason to hurt Cesaria. She was perfect. She was a single mother, a private-school teacher, and an actress in community theater. She had her life together, and I adored her.

Repeating the Cycle

For the first few years, life with Cesaria was wonderful. After we got married we moved in with her mother while our new house was being built. But one night in December 2001, Cesaria's ex-boyfriend stopped by unexpectedly—and I nearly ruined everything.

I stood, glaring, in the livingroom doorway as Cesaria invited him in, hugging him and kissing him on the cheek. As they sat down on the couch together, I felt a surge of fear. This guy was young, blonde, and blue-eyed; I was a 40-year-old Native American with brown eyes and black hair. How could Cesaria love me, compared with him? I knew she was going to run off with him.

Watching them, my fear and self-doubt turned to rage. I could feel veins pulsing in my neck. My hands were sweaty. I got tunnel vision. I'd never felt this way with Cesaria before.

Her ex didn't stay long, and after he left, I started an argument about his visit. But it went nowhere, so we just went to bed in silence.

At first, I lay there staring at the shadows on the wall. Then, suddenly, I exploded. I jumped on my wife—grabbing her, choking her, slapping her, pulling her hair.

"Duane!" Cesaria cried out, shocked. It was as if she was calling for my help—except I was the one attacking her.

You brought this on yourself, Cesaria, I thought. Out loud I threatened, "You don't have a good reason to live. I'm going to kill you." I wanted her to believe me, to be more scared than she'd ever been. Her fear would erase mine.

By the time I finished beating my tiny, 4'11" wife, she was bloody and bruised. I'd ruptured her eardrum and fractured her jaw. One of her ribs was torn away from the muscle.

At last, my anger was spent. I picked up my loaded gun and handed it over to her. "Here. Now its even," I said. "You've got the gun, so let's have a discussion."

When Cesaria's eyes met mine, I recoiled. She looked so afraid. My other wives had always stared at me like, "You're such a jerk." But Cesaria's wounded look was heartbreaking. For once, I was unable to justify what I'd done.

Owning Up to the Abuse

I avoided Cesaria the next morning by going to work early. At around
noon, she called to tell me she'd filed a report against me. I hung up.
As a detective, I knew I was going to be arrested. The evidence was all
over her face and body. I was about to lose everything—my wife, my
career, my friends—and I'd done it with my own hands. I thought
about killing myself. Or running away. I felt so guilty. I just wanted to
hold Cesaria—and I couldn't.

But I didn't run. Before the day's end, I was sitting in jail. I spent
four days there, thinking about what I'd done. Maybe I was to blame
for my failed marriages. Maybe it wasn't the fault of the women in my
life. On the day I was released, I went for a drive. My wife and children
were gone, and as I stared at the stuffed animal and baseball glove in
the backseat of my car—reminders of my family—I felt hopeless.

I was put on paid administrative leave following Cesaria's report,
but my lawyer warned me, "Your law-enforcement career is over." I
resigned and began working for a private investigator. I went about
my life in a daze for two weeks—and then Cesaria called.

We agreed to meet at a Denny's at midnight. I was so nervous—I
wanted her to trust me again. As I slipped into the booth, I noticed
she was wringing her hands. Her cell phone was on the table.

She stared at me, searching. I held her stare, silently trying to tell
her I knew I was wrong.

"Why did you hit me?" she asked.

"You were being disrespectful," I said, fumbling. "I felt like you
were going to leave me, and I didn't want you to go."

"Uh-uh," she said sternly. "Why did you hit me?"

"No more angry outbursts," I promised. "No more shouting. Everything will be OK."

"No," she said. "I want you to tell me why."

"I don't have the answers," I finally admitted. "I need to find
them." We ended up talking for hours.

Breaking the Pattern

Cesaria didn't give up on me. I entered a 52-week batterers' intervention program, and we both read books on domestic violence. Reading
about how violence is passed down from father to son made me
rethink my childhood. Some days, my dad used to open the door of
our trailer home and shout obscenities, angry at the way he was
treated in the "white man's world." Then he'd break down in tears.
Many nights, he'd come home drunk. He'd slap me, throw me across
the room, and then go looking for my mom. Those nights, I was
really scared. I'd get angry and think, someday I'm going to be big,
and I'll get back at you.

After I grew up and left home, I thought of myself as a survivor of
my childhood. But once I started reading about domestic violence, I

realized that it wasn't enough to have survived. And my job with the police had only reinforced the notion that it was OK to control other people with force. It was all wrong. I had to break out of the pattern.

Cesaria agreed to a reconciliation, but she set firm ground rules. She drew up a contract stating that if I ever got violent again, she would get the house, the car, everything. We signed it in front of a notary public. As we rebuilt our relationship, Cesaria began formulating an idea. She wanted to help other victims of domestic abuse so that they'd never feel as alone as she had. She explained that after I'd beaten her, her friends and family didn't support her at all. I was surprised and sad—and I agreed that no woman should be shunned just because she's a victim of abuse.

In January 2002, Cesaria and I founded an outreach organization called Victory Over Domestic Abuse (VODA). At first, I stayed in the background while Cesaria set the agenda. But slowly, I started talking to women about why men hit. It was difficult trying to explain what I'd done, and what I was doing to ensure I never abused again. But in the end, it made me feel good to say, "I'm on the right track."

To date, VODA has provided nearly 300 victims of domestic violence with financial assistance, counseling, and other services. In addition, I've spoken about domestic violence to hundreds of men at local businesses and church groups. I haven't been abusive since . . . December [2001]—though sometimes when I'm frustrated, I find myself clenching my fists, ready to hit. But I resist the urge. Cesaria's attitude helps: If you're in a place where even hollering seems wrong, it's easier not to use violence.

I still don't have all the answers, but I know the questions need to be looked at in a hard light—every day. I used to train dogs on the police force, and I think of curing yourself of violence in the same way as getting over a dog bite. First, you have to open the wound and clean out any poisons. Then the wound has to heal from the inside out. And I will always need to keep opening the wound in order to remain violence-free.

CRUSADER ON WHEELS: REACHING OUT TO RURAL VICTIMS OF ABUSE

Susan Schindehette and Tom Duffy

In the following selection, *People* reporters Susan Schindehette and Tom Duffy present the story of Wynona Ward, the founder of a free legal service in Vermont called Have Justice—Will Travel, which provides battered women in isolated rural areas with legal aid and social services. Ward herself is a survivor of child sexual abuse and the daughter of a battered woman, the authors explain. Determined to rescue other families from the intergenerational cycle of violence that plagued her own, she went back to college in her forties and graduated from Vermont Law School. While working in a free legal clinic, the authors relate, she realized that many rural victims of domestic violence have limited access to lawyers or social service agencies. Schindehette and Duffy write that, by traveling throughout the state of Vermont each week, Ward is able to bring assistance directly to the homes of battered women who otherwise might have no place to turn for help.

Wynona Ward still carries vivid memories from her childhood in rural Vermont—of the violence and sexual abuse suffered at the hands of her late father, an alcoholic laborer who routinely molested her from the time she was 3 years old. Even worse, she says, was seeing the beatings that her mother endured—and the indifference of the world around her. "When the neighbors heard screaming, they turned their heads," recalls Ward, 51. "It was devastating, but as a child I accepted it as the way it was."

Today she no longer does. As the founder of a free legal service called Have Justice—Will Travel, Ward doesn't just represent battered women in court. She also helps clients who might otherwise have no way of getting to lawyers or social-service agencies by traveling hundreds of miles a week in the backwaters of her home state in a 1996 Ford Explorer equipped with cell phone, laptop and portable printer. Dispensing advice on everything from restraining orders to auto loans, she sees to it that her clients, most of whom no longer live with their abusers, are making ends meet. "Sitting in her kitchen and talking with a woman, I can see what she needs," says Ward. "Does she have food? Heat? Do her kids need mittens?"

For battered women, such empathy is crucial. "Wynona told me I'd be okay, and I believed her," says Connie Button, 35, who ended an abusive relationship with Ward's help in 1999. "She has this way about her, a mothering quality."

Breaking the Cycle of Violence

The third of five children who grew up on a dirt road in east-central Vermont, Ward experienced her father's abuse as "a betrayal, something that makes you feel powerless," she says. "For years I blamed myself, that it was my fault and I should have stopped it." At 18 she escaped by marrying Harold Ward, now 51, a long-distance trucker she had dated since eighth grade. She worked as a secretary and took classes at Boston University, but in 1979, when Harold needed help on the road, she volunteered. For the next 15 years, the two worked as a team, hauling freight through the U.S. and Canada in their Diamond Reo 18-wheeler.

Then, in 1986, Ward's sister called to say that their father had molested a young family member. "The girl was the same age I was when he started," says Ward, whose fight to see her father prosecuted was thwarted because the girl was not deemed a credible witness. Five years later she learned that the same girl had again been molested—this time by Ward's brother Richard, then 41. In conversations with her sisters Ward discovered that two of them had also been abused by her father, who died in 2000, and that Richard had been molested by a relative. By that time, Ward recalls, she had learned that intergenerational abuse is often kept secret within families. "When the incident happened with my brother, I said, 'This has to stop.'"

In 1992, thanks in part to her efforts, her brother was sentenced to prison, where he died in 1997. But Ward didn't stop at that. She enrolled in a special program at Vermont College, and in two years earned her bachelor's degree, all the while driving cross-country with Harold. She went on to Vermont Law School, where, working in a free legal clinic, she saw that many abused women failed to follow through after getting restraining orders against their husbands. Such women, she realized, need not only legal counsel but a way out of their isolation. So in 1998, months after graduating, she launched Have Justice—Will Travel. Its goals: "First, break the generational cycle of violence. Second, help women become independent so their children see that Mommy isn't going to be beat up anymore."

Changing the World

Along with her road work, Ward operates a support group whose eight members meet weekly in the six-room house that Ward shares with

Harold and their five cats in Vershire, Vt. "These women aren't statistics to Wynona," says her husband. "They're extended family." Billi Gosh, founder of the Vermont Women's Fund, calls her "the Green Mountain Joan of Arc. She's truly changing the world."

Although a grant [in 2002] from the Department of Justice has allowed Ward to hire two additional attorneys, she still rises at 4 A.M. and puts in 80-hour weeks. "Sometimes I miss traveling to other parts of the country. It was wonderful," she says of her trucking days. "But when all is said and done, what I really want to remember is that I helped people. I helped them get away from abuse."

ORGANIZATIONS TO CONTACT

The editors have compiled the following list of organizations concerned with the issues presented in this book. The descriptions are derived from materials provided by the organizations. All have publications or information available for interested readers. The list was compiled on the date of publication of the present volume; the information provided here may change. Be aware that many organizations take several weeks or longer to respond to inquiries, so allow as much time as possible.

American Bar Association Commission on Domestic Violence
740 15th St. NW, Washington, DC 20005-1022
(202) 662-1000 • (202) 662-1744 • fax: (202) 662-1594
e-mail: cdv@staff.abanet.org • website: www.abanet.org.

The commission researches model domestic violence programs in an effort to develop a blueprint for a national multidisciplinary domestic violence program. The commission provides information on domestic violence law and offers numerous publications, including the brochure *Teen Dating Violence: There Is No Excuse*, the videotape *It's Not O.K.: Let's Talk About Domestic Violence*, and the books *The Impact of Domestic Violence on Your Legal Practice: A Lawyer's Handbook* and *A Guide for Employers: Domestic Violence in the Workplace.*

Center for Women Policy Studies (CWPS)
1211 Connecticut Ave. NW, Suite 312, Washington, DC 20036
(202) 872-1770 • fax: (202) 296-8962
e-mail: cwps@centerwomenpolicy.org • website: www.centerwomenpolicy.org

CWPS is an independent feminist policy research and advocacy organization. The center studies policies affecting the social, legal, health, and economic status of women. Available publications include the reports "Violence Against Disabled Women," "Violence Against Women as Bias-Motivated Hate Crime: Defining the Issues," and "Women with HIV/AIDS Speak Out on Domestic Violence."

Emerge: Counseling and Education to Stop Domestic Violence
2464 Massachusetts Ave., Suite 101, Cambridge, MA 02140
(617) 547-9879 • fax: (617) 547-0904
e-mail: emergedv@aol.com • website: www.emergedv.com

Emerge is a victim-advocacy organization that works to prevent domestic violence by providing training workshops to counselors and counseling services to batterers. It also conducts research and disseminates information. Publications available from Emerge include the articles "The Addicted or Alcoholic Batterer," "Working with Lesbian Batterers," and "Why Do Men Batter Their Wives?"

Family Violence Prevention Fund (FVPF)
383 Rhode Island St., Suite 304, San Francisco, CA 94103-5133
(415) 252-8900 • fax: (415) 252-8991
e-mail: info@endabuse.org • website: www.endabuse.org

FVPF is a national nonprofit organization concerned with domestic violence education, prevention, and public policy reform. It works to improve health care for battered women and to strengthen the judicial system's capacity to respond appropriately to domestic violence cases. The fund publishes a biannual newsletter, brochures, press releases, and informative packets on domestic violence such as "Responding to Domestic Violence in Lesbian, Gay, Transgender, and Bisexual (LGTB) Communities" and "Violence Against Women with Disabilities."

Independent Women's Forum (IWF)
1726 M St. NW, Suite 1001, Washington, DC 20036
(202) 419-1820
e-mail: info@iwf.org • website: www.iwf.org

The forum is a conservative women's advocacy group that believes in individual freedom and personal responsibility and promotes common sense over feminist ideology. It maintains that the incidence of domestic violence is exaggerated and that the Violence Against Women Act is ineffective and unjust. IWF publishes the *Women's Quarterly*.

National Center for Victims of Crime (NCVC)
2000 M St. NW, Suite 480, Washington, DC 20036
(202) 467-8700 • helpline: (800) FYI-CALL • fax: (202) 467-8701
e-mail: mail@ncvc.org • website: www.ncvc.org

NCVC is dedicated to serving individuals, families, and communities harmed by crime. The center provides direct aid to victims, as well as training and technical assistance to victim service organizations, counselors, lawyers, and criminal justice agencies. It also works for the passage of legislation to create resources and secure protection for victims of crime. NCVC's publications include a fact sheet on domestic violence, the report "Creating an Effective Stalking Protocol," and the quarterly journal *Victim Advocate*.

National Coalition Against Domestic Violence (NCADV)
PO Box 18749, Denver, CO 80218
(303) 839-1852 • fax: (303) 831-9251
e-mail: mainoffice@ncadv.org • website: www.ncadv.org

NCADV represents organizations and individuals that assist battered women and their children. It serves as a national information and referral network on domestic violence issues. The coalition sponsors programs to raise awareness about the campaign against domestic violence, develops and distributes educational products and publications, and works to influence public policy concerning battered women. Among its publications are the quarterly newsletter *Grassroots Connection*, the triannual *VOICE: The Journal of the Battered Women's Movement*, the information packet "Every Home a Safe Home," and the handbook *Teen Dating Violence Resource Manual*.

National Resource Center on Domestic Violence (NRCDV)
6400 Flank Dr., Suite 1300, Harrisburg, PA 17112-2791
(800) 537-2238 • fax: (717) 545-9456
website: www.nrcdv.org

NRCDV focuses on civil and criminal justice issues, child protection and custody issues, and health care access for battered women and their children. The center works to expand the service capacity of community-based domestic violence programs and state coalitions and assists government agencies, policy leaders, and other supporters of victims of domestic violence. Publications include brochures in Spanish and English, information packets, the paper "Strategies to Expand Battered Women's Economic Opportunities," and the report "Forging New Collaborations Between Domestic Violence Programs, Child Welfare Services, and Communities of Color."

Nicole Brown Charitable Foundation

PO Box 3777, Dana Point, CA 92629
(949) 283-5330
e-mail: info@nbcf.org • website: www.nbcf.org

Named for Nicole Brown Simpson, a victim of domestic violence, the foundation is dedicated to the eradication of family and partner violence. It strives to raise public awareness about the dangers of domestic violence through lectures and workshops. In addition, the foundation is committed to developing long-term transitional housing and life-skills programs for battered women and their children. It distributes informational packets on a variety of topics, including myths and facts about domestic violence, warning signs of teen dating violence, and batterer treatment programs.

NOW Legal Defense and Education Fund (NOW LDEF)

395 Hudson St., New York, NY 10014
(212) 925-6635 • fax: (212) 226-1066
e-mail: peo@nowldef.org • website: www.nowldef.org

NOW LDEF is a branch of the National Organization for Women (NOW). It is dedicated to the eradication of sex discrimination through litigation and public education. The organization publishes several legal resource kits on rape, stalking, and domestic violence, as well as information on the Violence Against Women Act. Among its other publications are numerous reports and studies, including "Report from the Front Lines: The Impact of Violence on Poor Women" and "The Impact of Violence in the Lives of Working Women: Creating Solutions, Creating Change."

U.S. Department of Justice

Office on Violence Against Women
810 7th St. NW, Washington, DC 20531
(202) 307-6026 • hotline: (800) 799-SAFE • fax: (202) 307-3911
website: www.ojp.usdoj.gov/vawo

The office is responsible for the overall coordination and focus of the Justice Department's efforts to combat violence against women. It leads a comprehensive national effort to combine tough new federal laws with assistance to states and localities to fight domestic violence and other crimes against women. The office's publications include the reports "Stalking and Domestic Violence" and "Intimate Partner Violence."

BIBLIOGRAPHY

Books

Eve S. Buzawa and
and Carl G. Buzawa — *Domestic Violence: The Criminal Justice Response.* Thousand Oaks, CA: Sage, 2003.

Clare Dalton and
Elizabeth M. Schneider — *Battered Women and the Law.* New York: Foundation Press, 2001.

Meg Kennedy Dugan
and Roger R. Hock — *It's My Life Now: Starting Over After an Abusive Relationship or Domestic Violence.* New York: Routledge, 2000.

Ann Jones — *Next Time, She'll Be Dead: Battering and How to Stop It.* Boston, MA: Beacon Press, 2000.

Alyce D. LaViolette
and Ola W. Barnett — *It Could Happen to Anyone: Why Battered Women Stay.* Thousand Oaks, CA: Sage, 2000.

Elizabeth Dermody
Leonard — *Convicted Survivors: The Imprisonment of Battered Women Who Kill.* Albany: State University of New York Press, 2002.

Mary Marecek — *Breaking Free from Partner Abuse: Voices of Battered Women Caught in the Cycle of Domestic Violence.* Buena Park, CA: Morning Glory Press, 1999.

Albert R. Roberts, ed. — *Handbook of Domestic Violence Intervention Strategies: Policies, Programs, and Legal Remedies.* New York: Oxford University Press, 2002.

Linda P. Rouse — *You Are Not Alone: A Guide for Battered Women.* Holmes Beach, FL: Learning, 2000.

Wendy Smooth and
Leslie R. Wolfe — *Violence Against Women and Girls—Research and Data in Brief.* Washington, DC: Center for Women Policy Studies, 1999.

Lenore E.A. Walker — *The Battered Woman Syndrome.* New York: Springer, 2000.

Susan Weitzman — *"Not to People Like Us": Hidden Abuse in Upscale Marriages.* New York: Basic Books, 2000.

Michele Weldon — *I Closed My Eyes: Revelations of a Battered Woman.* Center City, MN: Hazelden, 1999.

Carolyn M. West, ed. — *Violence in the Lives of Black Women: Battered, Black, and Blue.* New York: Haworth Press, 2002.

Periodicals

Deborah K. Anderson
and Daniel G. Saunders — "Leaving an Abusive Partner," *Trauma, Violence, and Abuse,* April 2003.

Ileana Arias et al. — "Violence Against Women: The State of Batterer Prevention Programs," *Journal of Law, Medicine and Ethics,* Fall 2002.

Louise Bill — "The Victimization and Revictimization of Female Offenders," *Corrections Today*, December 1998.

Mark Blackburn — "Know Thyself," *Ms.*, October/November 2001.

Diane Boudreau — "A Matter of Rape," *ASU Research Magazine*, Fall 2000.

Larken Bradley — "My Line in the Sand," *Ms.*, October/November 2001.

Cesar Chelala — "A Hidden Epidemic: Gender Violence," *Américas*, July/August 2003.

Sarah Childress — "9/11's Hidden Toll: Muslim-American Women Are Quietly Coping with a Tragic Side Effect of the Attacks—a Surge in Domestic Violence," *Newsweek*, August 4, 2003.

Annia Ciezadlo — "Failure to Protect," *City Limits*, September/October 2000.

Ann Coulter — "Annie's Got Her Gun," *George*, August 1999.

Jane Drucker — "Lesbian Domestic Violence," *Lesbian News*, April 2003.

Cara Feinberg — "Hitting Home: Domestic Violence Is the Issue That Embarrasses Traditionalists," *American Prospect*, April 8, 2002.

Martha Finney and Deborah Prussel — "Shattered Lives," *Across the Board*, October 2000.

Jan Goodwin — "The Ultimate Growth Industry: Trafficking in Women and Girls," *On the Issues*, Fall 1998.

August Gribbin — "Congress Targets Traffic of Sex Slaves into U.S.," *Insight*, August 2, 1999.

Jacky Hardy — "Everything Old Is New Again: The Use of Gender-Based Terrorism Against Women," *Minerva: Quarterly Report on Women and the Military*, Summer 2001.

Rachel Jewkes — "Intimate Partner Violence: Causes and Prevention," *Lancet*, April 20, 2002.

G. Krantz — "Violence Against Women: A Global Public Health Issue," *Journal of Epidemiology and Community Health*, April 2002.

Paul Mandelbaum — "Dowry Deaths in India: Let Only Your Corpse Come Out of That House," *Commonweal*, October 8, 1999.

Marie Claire — "One in Three Women Will Be Abused in Her Lifetime," October 2003.

Tonya McCormick — "Convicting Domestic Violence Abusers When the Victim Remains Silent," *BYU Journal of Public Law*, Fall 1999.

Jennifer L. Pozner — "Not All Domestic Violence Studies Are Created Equal," *Extra*, November/December 1999.

Scott Raab — "Men Explode," *Esquire*, September 2000.

Simon Robinson — "The Last Rites," *Time International*, December 3, 2001.

Jennie Ruby   "It's Time to Stop Tolerating Rape," *Off Our Backs*,
                          September/October 2002.

Dean Schillinger   "In Opposition to Mandatory Reporting," *Western*
and Ariella Hyman   *Journal of Medicine*, August 1999.

Andrea Smith   "Keeping Safe: Native Women Mobilize Their Own
                          Coalition Against Domestic Violence," *ColorLines,*
                          Summer 2002.

Silja J.A. Talvi   "The Suffering Within: The Plight of Battered Women
                          Who Kill in Self-Defense," *Z Magazine*, October 2002.

Lauren R. Taylor   "The Home Front," *Government Executive*, March 2002.

Stacy A. Teicher   "How Violence at Home Is Felt at Work," *Christian
                          Science Monitor*, September 15, 2003.

INDEX